T0148958

# BATTLE OF
# THE BULGE
# 1944-45

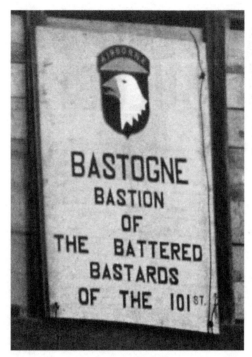

*A dark sense of humour prevailed during the siege of Bastogne. (NARA 111-SC-226804)*

# BATTLE OF THE BULGE 1944-45

ANDREW RAWSON

Cover illustrations. Front: *Men of the 2nd Division hug the sides of a shallow ditch as German shells rain down on their positions on Elsenborn Ridge (NARA 111-SC-197304).* Back: *Gls of the 26th Division during the attack on Wiltz (NARA 111-SC-199092).*

First published 2011 as *Battle Story: Battle of the Bulge 1944–45*
This edition first published 2022

The History Press
97 St George's Place, Cheltenham,
Gloucestershire, GL50 3QB
www.thehistorypress.co.uk

© The History Press, 2011, 2022

The right of Andrew Rawson to be identified as the Author
of this work has been asserted in accordance with the
Copyright, Designs and Patents Act 1988.

Andrew Rawson has asserted his moral right to be identified
as the Author of this Work.

All rights reserved. No part of this book may be reprinted
or reproduced or utilised in any form or by any electronic,
mechanical or other means, now known or hereafter invented,
including photocopying and recording, or in any information
storage or retrieval system, without the permission in writing
from the Publishers.

British Library Cataloguing in Publication Data.
A catalogue record for this book is available from the British Library.

ISBN 978 1 80399 051 4

Typesetting and origination by The History Press
Printed and bound in Great Britain by TJ Books Limited, Padstow, Cornwall.

**MIX**
Paper from
responsible sources
**FSC** www.fsc.org **FSC® C013056**

Trees for LYfe

# CONTENTS

# Battle of the Bulge 1944–45

*The bullet-scarred sign went back to Fort Campbell. (NARA 111-SC-200445)*

# INTRODUCTION

On the morning of 6 June 1944 Allied troops made airborne and seaborne landings on the coast of Normandy and by nightfall they had established a slender beachhead. The long awaited battle for the Second Front had started and over the next six weeks the British and Commonwealth soldiers serving under Field Marshal Bernard Montgomery and the American soldiers under General Omar Bradley fought to expand their foothold in Nazi-occupied Europe.

While the British drew in German reserves around the town of Caen, the Americans fought inch by inch through the Normandy bocage as reinforcements poured into the beachhead. Finally, the breakthrough came on 25 July when First US Army launched Operation *Cobra*. As Montgomery's 21st Army Group advanced south from Caen, Bradley's 12th Army Group pushed south to Avranches before turning east in a huge arc to try and encircle Army Group B. General Eisenhower's plan nearly worked and large numbers of Field Marshal Walter Model's men were trapped in what became known as the battle for the Falaise Pocket.

The Allied Armies advanced quickly across France while the remnants of OB West fell back in disorder towards Germany and the safety of the West Wall (also known as the Siegfried Line), a long line of fortifications along the border, the Allied Armies followed as fast as they could. While Montgomery's 21st Army Group entered Belgium and entered Brussels on the north flank, Bradley advanced east, liberating Paris before heading towards the German border. Following a second successful Allied landing in southern France General Jacob Devers' 6th Army Group pushed quickly up the Rhône Valley and linked up with Bradley's advance. However, while progress was exceeding all expectations the advance started to falter by mid September because of mounting difficulties in keeping the front line troops supplied. The Germans either held onto ports or destroyed them, leaving the Allies reliant on bringing supplies over the beaches. The destruction of the French rail network meant that everything had to be moved by lorry. With summer turning to autumn, Eisenhower was concerned that his Armies would find themselves stranded in front of the Siegfried Line at the end of a tenuous supply line.

An attempt to outflank the fortified line by pushing through Holland was suggested by Montgomery and approved; on 17 September Operation *Market Garden* was launched. The plan was to cross the Maas, Waal, and Rhine rivers in southern Holland using British and American airborne troops to pave the way for the ground troops but after a fleeting glimpse of success, German reserves moved in to stop 21st Army Group just short of its final objective. The failure to cross the Rhine left Eisenhower needing to reconsider his options.

An attempt on Hitler's life in the Wolf's Lair on 20 July 1944 and the subsequent purge of the Armed Forces High Command, in which many senior officers were executed, had made the Führer paranoid. The purge had gone right to the top and Generalfeldmarschall Günther von Kluge committed suicide when implicated in the plot.

With the Soviet Armies winning the battle for the Eastern front, Hitler wanted to focus on defeating the Allies in the West and on 31 July the Führer made the declaration that the war had to be won in the West and that the Allied armies had to be stopped from breaking out of Normandy. The *Wehrmacht* could not halt them and over the next six weeks they advanced across France and Belgium. As the Allied advance ground to a halt on Germany's border, Hitler conceived the offensive in the Ardennes; a counterattack designed to win the war.

The day before Operation *Market Garden* was launched, OKW's staff were holding a briefing at Hitler's headquarters in East Prussia, a place known as the Wolf's Lair. General Alfred Jodl, OKW's Chief of Operations Staff, was explaining the situation on the Western Front and it was looking bad for *Wehrmacht*. Allied divisions outnumbered the Germans by two to one and the Americans had just crossed the German border at Aachen. As he went on to describe how most divisions were short of manpower, armour, heavy weapons and ammunition, Hitler interrupted and announced; 'I have just made a momentous decision. I shall go over to the counterattack, here, out of the Ardennes, with the objective – Antwerp.'

Hitler also had a new Commander in Chief, West, to plan the offensive following Kluge's suicide. On 1 September Field Marshal Gerd von Rundstedt took command having been sacked two months earlier for urging Hitler to make peace following the D-Day landings on the Normandy coast. He was ordered to stall the Allied advance across France and Belgium to give time for the West Wall to be strengthened. Meanwhile, secret planning to gather enough men, armour, artillery and ammunition to smash through the Allied line began immediately. It was going to take a tremendous effort to prepare for the offensive but the stakes were high; the survival of the Nazi regime depended on the Wehrmacht's success.

*Jodl, Hitler and Rundstedt; while Hitler conceived Operation* Wacht am Rhein, *Jodl and Rundstedt argued over the pros and cons of the Big Solution and the Small Solution.*

# TIMELINES

## European Campaign: 6 June 1944 to 8 May 1945

**1944**

| | |
|---|---|
| **6 June** | Operation *Overlord*: D-Day, Allied airborne and seaborne landings on the north coast of France begins. The bloody battle through the Normandy bocage follows. |
| **25 July** | Operation *Cobra*: The Allies breakout into open country begins. |
| **12–21 August** | The battle of the Falaise Pocket results in the destruction of a large part of Army Group B; the race across France begins. |
| **15 August** | Operation *Dragoon*: The Allies land on the south coast of France and move quickly north up the Rhône valley. |
| **Early September** | 21st Army Group advances quickly across north France and into Belgium while 12th Army Group advances to the German border; Allied advance halted by a stretched line of communications while Germans seek safety behind the West Wall. |

# Timelines

| | |
|---|---|
| 12 September | Third and Seventh Armies link up at Chantillon-sur-Seine. |
| 14 September | The start of the bloody five-month-long battle for the Hürtgen Forest. |
| 17–25 September | Operation *Market Garden*: 21st Army Group uses airborne and ground troops to advance through southern Holland. Although Montgomery's troops cross the Rivers Maas and Waal, they fail to secure a bridgehead across Rhine River at Arnhem. |
| 2–21 October | The fierce battle for Aachen, the first German city to be captured |
| 16 December | Operation *Wacht am Rhein*: The start of the Battle of the Bulge in the Ardennes. |
| 27 January | Official end of the Battle of the Bulge. |
| 8 February–5 March | The battle of the Reichswald and the advance to the Rhine, including Operation *Veritable* and Operation *Grenade*. |
| 7 March | First Crossing of the Rhine River at Remagen. |
| Late March | Multiple crossings of the Rhine in Third and Seventh Army areas. 21st Army Group launches Operation *Varsity* crossing the river around Wesel; Operation *Plunder*, advancing north of the Ruhr. |
| April | Rapid advances deep into the heart of Germany, as OB West's resistance collapses. |
| 25 April | US and Soviet troops meet at Torgau on the River Elbe, cutting Germany in two. |
| 30 April | Adolf Hitler commits suicide in the Führer Bunker in Berlin. |
| 8 May | Surrender of all remaining German armed forces. |

1944

1945

# Battle of the Bulge:
# 16 December 1944 to 16 January 1945

## 16–17 December

Operation *Wacht am Rhein* Begins

| | |
|---|---|
| **Sixth Panzer Army** | LXVII Corps stopped around Krinkelt and Rocherath while I SS Panzer Corps break through into the Amblève valley. |
| **Fifth Panzer Army** | LXVI Corps surrounds 106th Division on the Schnee Eifel while LVIII Panzer and XLVII Panzer Corps struggle to cross the River Our. |
| **Seventh Army** | LXXXV Corps keeps pace with Fifth Panzer Army but LXXX Corps struggles to cross the River Sauer. |

## 18–19 December

Army Group B's Breakthrough Begins

| | |
|---|---|
| **Sixth Panzer Army** | LXVII Corps unable to break V Corps around Elsenborn while I SS Panzer Corps is stopped in the Amblève valley. |
| **Fifth Panzer Army** | LXVI Corps runs into 7th Armored Division at St Vith while LVIII Panzer Corps breaks through 28th Division and advances past Houffalize; XLVII Panzer Corps battles with rearguards covering Bastogne. |
| **Seventh Army** | North flank of LXXXV Corps advances to Wiltz but the right flank stalls at Diekirch. LXXX Corps struggles to make progress on the west bank of Sauer. |
| **20 December** | SHAEF splits command of the Ardennes battlefield into two with 21st Army Group taking command of First Army in the north and 12th Army Group taking command of Third Army in the south. |

## 20–21 December

The Battles for St Vith and Bastogne

| | |
|---|---|
| **Sixth Panzer Army** | Attacks against Malmédy fail while Kampfgruppe Peiper is surrounded in the Amblève valley |

# Timelines

20–21 December

**Fifth Panzer Army**     LXVI Corps fails to capture St Vith and while LVIII Panzer Corps advances west of Houffalize, 101st Airborne Division reaches Bastogne before XLVII Panzer Corps does.

**Seventh Army**     III Corps prepare to counterattack Fifth Panzer Army's southern flank while XII Corps prepares to strike at Seventh Army.

## Army Group B's High Water Mark

22–23 December

**Sixth Panzer Army**     The St Vith salient is evacuated and Sixth Panzer Army attacks XVIII Airborne Corps between Vielsalm and Manhay.

**Fifth Panzer Army**     LVIII Panzer Corps fails to breakthrough around Hotton so it transfers west of the River Ourthe to face VII Corps positions around Marche. Part of XLVII Panzer Corps reaches Rochefort while the rest attacks Bastogne.

**Third US Army**     The counterattack starts and while III Corps advances towards Bastogne and the River Sure, XII Corps starts pushing Seventh Army back to the River Sauer.

## The Counteroffensive Intensifies

24–25 December

**Sixth Panzer Army**     Unable to break through XVIII Corps lines between Trois Ponts and Hotton.

**Fifth Panzer Army**     LVIII Panzer Corps is stopped in front of Marche while part of XLVII Panzer Corps is stopped close to Dinant and the Meuse. The rest of XLVII Panzer Corps is still engaged at Bastogne.

**Third US Army**     III Corps closes in on Bastogne and Wiltz while XII Corps moves closer to the River Sauer.

**26 December**     Army Group B's advance is over. Sixth Panzer Army calls off attacks while the tip of Fifth Panzer Army's is blunted by Allied counterattacks. III Corps reaches Bastogne and Army Group Lüttwitz prepares to counterattack. XII Corps forces Seventh Army back across the River Sauer.

# Battle of the Bulge 1944–45

| | |
|---|---|
| 27–29 December | III Corps wins the battle for the Bastogne corridor while Third Army prepares to increase the width of its counterattack. |
| 30 December | Third Army begins its counterattack west of Bastogne. |
| 2 January | Third Army begins its counterattack from Bastogne. |
| 3 January | First Army begins its counterattack against the north side of the salient. |
| 16 January | First and Third Armies meet in Houffalize. |

## MAP KEY

| | |
|---|---|
| ***ALLIED*** | Troop deployments (Italicised Bold) |
| **AXIS** | Troop deployments (Bold) |
| | Rivers |
| | Towns |
| | Siegfried Line |
| | Division deployment boundaries |
| | Combat line |
| | Axis frontlines |
| | Allied frontlines |
| | Axis advances |
| | Allied advances |

# HISTORICAL BACKGROUND

## Conceiving the Plan

Why was the Ardennes area so important to Hitler's plans? The Eastern Front was too extensive and the Soviet armies were too large for Germany to force an endgame in the east. While the Wehrmacht could afford to give up territory in the East, Hitler knew he would never be able to negotiate with Stalin. The Western Front was small enough for decisive action and Germany could not afford to lose the Ruhr, its industrial heartland, and the Allied armies were getting closer. The West Wall, a line of fortifications along its western border, was also an ideal position to hold with a thin crust of troops, allowing reserves to concentrate for the counteroffensive.

Hitler wanted to break through and then turn north, driving a wedge between the British and American armies. The advance would isolate British 21st Army Group in Holland from 12th US Army Group in Belgium, removing the threat to the Ruhr. The final objective was the port of Antwerp, which would be the Allies' main point of entry for supplies in Europe once the River Scheldt was opened to shipping. Its seizure would severely weaken SHAEF's situation on the Western Front and then negotiations with the Allies could begin. At least that was Hitler's plan.

By the middle of September it was an overstretched supply line rather than Rundstedt's capabilities or the tenacity of the German soldier which brought the Allied advance to a halt in front of the West Wall. While SS panzer divisions could be withdrawn immediately from the line, OKW West estimated that it would take until the end of October to withdraw the rest of the troops from the line. On hearing the news, Hitler set the target date for the attack as 1 November and he made it clear to Rundstedt that no ground must be given up in the meantime. It was a tall order for the new Commander in Chief.

## Reinforcing the Wehrmacht

By September 1944 Germany had suffered over three million military casualties and untold millions of civilian casualties. The Third Reich's cities and industries were under constant air attack but Reich Minister Albert Speer was working on expanding the economy. The people carried on working in spite of the devastation but while new factories sprung up in the countryside it was becoming increasingly difficult to meet the Armed Forces' needs. It seemed that only Hitler was optimistic about the Third Reich's capabilities to launch an offensive in the West.

Rundstedt must have wondered where the troops would come from to launch such an ambitious attack but plans were already underway to find them. On 19 August Hitler instructed Walter Buhle, OKW's Army Chief of Staff, and Speer to organise enough men and materiel for the November offensive. Heinrich Himmler was also appointed head of a new 'Replacement Army' and he assembled eighteen new divisions and ten panzer brigades by taking men from the military staff and the security services. Although only two of the divisions were sent to the Western Front most of the new tanks, assault guns and artillery manufactured in the summer were sent west.

Hitler had to adjust the timing of the attack until late November to allow the recruitment of another 25 new divisions for an 'operational reserve'. OKW assembled many by recalling units from the Balkans and Finland to the Western Front. Joseph Goebbels also instigated a 'comb-out program', expanding the conscription age limits while lowering medical standards for men recovering from battle injuries.

The Navy and Air Force were also combed for able-bodied men and even the Nazi Party faithful who had so far avoided military service were called up. Employment exemptions were rechecked, new non-essential jobs were announced and many industries and agriculture were investigated with a view to replacing workers with concentration camp inmates.

Hundreds of thousands of new conscripts were found and then formed into new *Volks Grenadier* Divisions rather than strengthening existing formations on Hitler's insistence. The expanding Wehrmacht was looking impressive on paper but many divisions were below strength or short of tanks, transport, artillery and all kinds of equipment. The problem was that Hitler believed they were all at full strength and anyone who disagreed was accused of defeatism or treason.

By the time Hitler made his announcement on 16 September, his paranoia had led him to be involved in every major military decision, even getting involved in detailed planning. However, the role of the Wehrmacht's Chief of the Operations Staff must not be underestimated. Jodl turned the Führer's ideas into military

Although the German generals dare not speak out against Hitler, in private they were scathing of his plans for the Ardennes Offensive. Rundstedt later admitted that 'all, absolutely all, conditions for the possible success of such an offensive were lacking.' Field Marshal Model's reaction was blunter; 'This plan hasn't got a damned leg to stand on.'

plans and then made sure they happened. He also represented the Wehrmacht commanders, presenting their suggestions and objections to Hitler.

## Jodl Draws up Hitler's Ideas

Around 25 September Jodl was ordered to turn Hitler's idea for a counteroffensive into an operational plan. The plan had to fulfil eight objectives:

1  The attack would be launched by Field Marshal Walter Model's Army Group B
2  The attack would be made in the Ardennes in late November
3  Success depended on secret planning, tactical surprise and a speedy advance
4  The initial objective was to cross the Meuse River between Liège and Namur
5  The final objective was to capture Antwerp, cutting the Allied line in two
6  Two panzer armies would spearhead the attack with an infantry army on each flank
7  The attack would be supported by the Luftwaffe and many artillery and rocket units
8  The plan was to destroy the British and Canadians north of the line Antwerp – Liège

The Chief of the OKW, Field Marshal Wilhelm Keitel, was hardly involved in the planning while Rundstedt was kept in the dark. Jodl did all of the work and came up with five alternatives:

1  Operation *Holland*: single-thrust from Venlo towards Antwerp
2  Operation *Liège-Aachen*: a double northwest thrust from northern Luxembourg and Aachen
3  Operation *Luxembourg*: a double attack from central Luxembourg and Metz towards Longwy

4  Operation *Lorraine*: a double attack from Metz and Baccarat towards Nancy
5  Operation *Alsace*: a double attack from Epinal and Montbeliard towards Vesoul

Operation *Liège-Aachen* was chosen and the main drive would be made through the Ardennes and Eifel areas. This double-pronged attack became known as the *Big Solution*. Jodl presented the outline plan on 19 October and three days later representatives from Rundstedt's and Model's forces were briefed about the operation at the Wolf's Lair.

Jodl's plan had Fifth Panzer and Sixth Panzer Armies leading Army Group B's attack while Seventh Army advanced in echelon on the south flank. Hitler promised eighteen infantry and twelve armoured (or mechanized) divisions and Hermann Göring promised maximum support from the Luftwaffe. Preparations had to be complete by 20 November ready to attack five days later. The timing was based on the high possibility of ten days of bad weather, in the hope it would cancel out Allied air supremacy.

*Army Group B's commander, Field Marshal Walter Model. It could be argued that Hitler could have transferred troops from the Eastern Front or shortened the Western Front to release men; he refused to do either. He was adamant that Antwerp was the goal and it had to be taken with his initial estimate of around thirty divisions.*

*The winter of 1944–45 was one of the coldest in living memory and American, British and German troops suffered in the terrible conditions; civilian refugees did too. Private Thomas O'Brien of the 26th Infantry Division tucks into his C Ration in a snow-covered field. (NARA 111-SC-198483)*

## The Generals' Reaction

Hitler had personally selected all Wehrmacht generals following the July Plot, choosing officers who were either subservient or hardened Nazis. None would, or even could, stand up against the Führer and he viewed their proposals and protests with suspicion. He was also involved in decision making at all levels and nothing could be changed without his permission, not even the movement of individual divisions.

While Rundstedt was an old school military general, Army Group B's commander, Field Marshal Walter Model, was a younger, politically motivated general. Relations between the two were frosty but they dealt with military matters in a workmanlike manner. However, the Führer's interference often meant that Rundstedt was often treated as a go-between, merely rubberstamping Army Group B's plans for approval by OKW.

Both Rundstedt and Model agreed that the objective was too ambitious for the troops available and that there was insufficient

> The Ardennes Offensive had two codenames. The one
> usually used was Operation *Watch on the Rhine (Wacht
> am Rhein)* but an alternative name was the *Defensive
> Battle in the West (Abwehrschlacht im Westen)*. Both
> options had been chosen to make them sound like
> defensive plans.

time to prepare for it. They were concerned that Army Group B would end up in a salient, with its flanks exposed to counterattack.

Rundstedt and Model submitted their alternative plans to OKW during a meeting at Army Group B's headquarters on 27 October and they had come to the same conclusion, presenting what would be called the *Small Solution*. Rundstedt's Plan *Martin* had Fifth Panzer and Sixth Panzer Armies advancing on a narrow (25-mile-wide) front, north of the line Huy-Antwerp. It avoided the rugged Ardennes terrain and the distance to the Meuse was shorter, while there was good tank country beyond the river. A secondary attack north of Aachen and aimed towards Liège would rip open the Allied line.

Model's Plan *Autumn Fog* was broader (40 miles wide), and it covered the north half of Hitler's front. There would no second attack to the north, and spare troops would follow in a second wave; Seventh Army would also attack later on the south flank. Following the discussion Model amended his plan to match Plan *Martin*.

Hitler's directive was delivered to Rundstedt on 2 November and Jodl's covering letter made it clear who was in charge: 'The venture for the far-flung objective [Antwerp] is unalterable although, from a strictly technical standpoint, it appears to be disproportionate to our available forces. In our present situation, however, we must not shrink from staking everything on one card.' Rundstedt replied with his concerns about the shortage of troops and his doubts about the Wehrmacht's ability to hold on unless the US armies could be destroyed.

Arguments and discussions comparing the Small Solution against the Big Solution followed and while Hitler thought the Small Solution was too small, the generals believed they had insufficient resources for the Big Solution. There would be only one winner; the Führer.

Rundstedt also wanted a simultaneous two-pronged assault, to increase the impact of the offensive. Hitler disagreed and OKW's operations directive on 10 November forbade one. Although Rundstedt considered making a secondary attack from the Venlo area once the Allies started moving their reserves to the Ardennes, XII SS Corps was too weak to carry it out.

While Hitler's plans were coming to fruition in November, the Allies intervened with their own offensives and as Third US Army attacked in the Metz sector, First and Ninth US Armies attacked east of Aachen. During the Battle of the Hürtgen Forest it was obvious that divisions were being prevented from withdrawing to refit ready for the Ardennes. Rundstedt and Model believed that success at Aachen promised tactical success and they proposed counterattacking: 'A surprise attack directed against the weakened enemy, after the conclusion of his unsuccessful breakthrough attempts in the greater Aachen area, offers the greatest chance of success.' Hitler replied: 'Preparations for an improvisation will not be made.'

On 26 November Rundstedt and Model were still asking Jodl to change to the Small Solution but Hitler would not budge. Model even took his Panzer Army commanders, Joseph Dietrich of Sixth Panzer Army and Hasso von Manteuffel of Panzer Army, to Berlin to petition the Führer to change his mind on 2 December. He refused again. Four days later Rundstedt and Model submitted a final draft of their operations order detailing a second attack; Hitler again rejected the suggestion. He approved the final version of the operations order for *Wacht am Rhein* three days later. It was virtually the same plan that the Führer had conceived three months earlier.

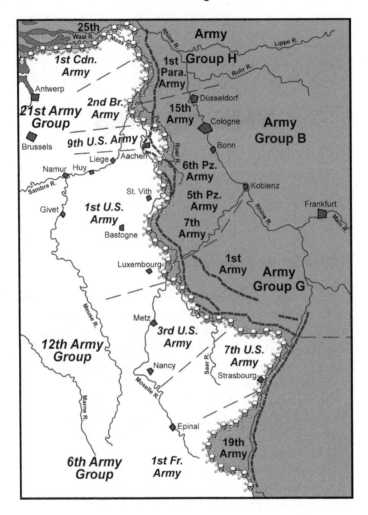

A summary of the situation on the Western Front at the beginning of December 1944. Army Group B had gathered three armies and aimed to cross the River Meuse between Liège and Givet before turning northwest towards Antwerp.

# THE ARMIES

## The Ardennes Battlefield

Hitler's chosen battlefield included some of the most difficult terrain on the Western Front. German troops had passed through it twice already, in August 1914 and May 1940, but they had advanced unopposed and during good weather on both occasions. The question was could mechanized forces move quickly through the Ardennes' forested hills in the middle of winter?

The northeast part of the battlefield is known as the Eifel and it has many villages and good roads running through its forests. The ridges east of St Vith are known as the Schnee Eifel and the West Wall fortifications ran along their summit. To the east of Liège is the Hohes Venn, an area dotted with lakes and marshes.

In the north is the open and rolling countryside of the Low Ardennes. The Upper Ourthe valley is known as the Famenne Depression and it extends west through Marche and Rochefort to the River Meuse at Givet and Dinant. The High Ardennes to the south has many ridges and hills interspersed with narrow valleys and ravines. It is also dotted with villages and a patchwork of woods and forests. Control of the Ardennes road network was essential for success. There were few good roads and towns where they met, such as Malmédy and St Vith in the north and Bastogne and St Hubert in the south, had to be taken quickly so that supply columns could keep up with the advance. Most of the roads wound their way through narrow valleys or forests and they would force troops into columns to cross rivers and negotiate ravines. Traffic jams were likely and the anticipated poor weather would make them worse.

## The German Commanders

### Generalfeldmarschall Gerd von Rundstedt (1875–1953), commander of Oberbefehlshaber West (OB West)

Von Rundstedt was recalled to active service to command Army Group South during the invasion of Poland in September 1939 and he then commanded the invasion force which overran France in May 1940. After taking part in the planning of Operation *Sealöwe*, the invasion of England, he was given orders to develop the coastal defences of France and the Low Countries.

Von Rundstedt transferred to the Eastern Front in 1941, commanding Army Group South during its part in the invasion of the Soviet Union, codenamed Operation *Barbarossa*. Having led his troops deep into Soviet territory, he was sacked by Hitler in November 1941 after asking permission to withdraw from the Rostov area.

*OKW West's commander, Field Marshal Gerd von Rundstedt.*

Hitler recalled von Rundstedt to duty in March 1942, placing him once again in command of the west. He failed to develop the Atlantic Wall, refusing to believe the Allies would land in Normandy and did not act on Field Marshal Erwin Rommel's advice to deploy his armoured reserve close to the coast. These decisions would cost OB West dearly and after the Normandy invasion in June 1944 von Rundstedt was sacked for daring to urge Hitler to negotiate with the Allies.

Von Rundstedt's replacement, Generalfeldmarschall Günther von Kluge committed suicide in August after being implicated in the July plot to assassinate the Führer. Von Rundstedt was reappointed as the Allied Armies advanced. His first two tasks were to hold onto the West Wall and plan for a counter offensive in the Ardennes. Over the next three months he was at loggerheads with Hitler over the feasibility of Operation *Wacht am Rhein*.

## Generalfeldmarshall Walter Model (1891–1945), commander of Army Group B

Model served as a chief of staff during the invasions of Poland and France but was given command of 3rd Panzer Division in November 1940, playing a leading part in Operation *Barbarossa* the following summer. He was promoted quickly and took command of XLI Panzer Corps as it attacked Moscow in October 1941 and Ninth Army in the Rzhev Salient the following January. His Army evacuated the salient in March 1943 and four months later Model was playing a leading part in the Battle of Kursk.

Model took command of Army Group North in January 1944, carrying out a fighting withdrawal from the Leningrad front. He did the same in command of Army Group North Ukraine in the spring and with Army Group Centre in the summer, becoming Hitler's favoured trouble shooter during the Soviet onslaught. Model transferred to the Western Front in August, taking over Army Group B as it faced annihilation in the Falaise Pocket. Although he briefly commanded OB West following Kluge's suicide, he returned to Army Group B and spent the autumn rebuilding it ready for Operation *Wacht am Rhein*.

> The *Volks Grenadier* Divisions were formed from younger and older men, using a cadre of returning wounded soldiers to train them. Although were at full strength in manpower, they were often short of weapons, armour and artillery, making them much weaker than a standard infantry division.

## The Allied Commanders

### General Dwight D. Eisenhower (1890–1969), Supreme Allied Commander of the Allied Expeditionary Force (SHAEF)

Eisenhower spent the first seven months of the war in Washington, first as Deputy Chief in charge of Pacific Defenses and then Chief of the War Plans Division. He then served as Assistant Chief of Staff heading the new Operations Division under Chief of Staff General George C. Marshall.

In June 1942 Eisenhower was appointed Commanding General, European Theater of Operations (ETOUSA) and in November 1942 also became Supreme Commander Allied (Expeditionary) Force of the North African Theater of Operations (NATOUSA) through the new operational Allied (Expeditionary) Force Headquarters (A(E) FHQ). He gave up command of ETOUSA to command NATOUSA and following the capitulation of Axis forces in North Africa, his command captured Sicily and invaded the Italian peninsula.

Eisenhower resumed command of ETOUSA in January 1944 and was appointed Supreme Allied Commander of the Allied Expeditionary Force a month later, taking over responsibility for planning the invasion of Normandy, France, in June, the operation codenamed *Overlord*. He was commander of the successful invasion of northern France, the eventual breakout across France, taking

*Neither Eisenhower nor Bradley leader believed the Germans possessed the material or men to launch an offensive. It is smiles all round as the two generals discuss their own plans with General Louis Craig of 9th Infantry Division. (NARA 111-SC-199344)*

control of the forces which took part in the southern invasion in August. Eisenhower remained in command of all Allied forces until the end of the war, weathering the difficult battles for the West Wall, the Battle of the Bulge and the final drive into the heart of Germany. His command of ETOUSA, gave him administrative command of all US forces on the Western Front, stretching from the North Sea coast to the Alps.

### General Omar N. Bradley (1893–1981), commander of 12th Army Group

Bradley's first combat experience came in early in 1943 when he served as Eisenhower's trouble-shooter in North Africa after the disastrous battle of the Kasserine Pass. He commanded II Corps during the final Tunisian battles in April and May and then during the July invasion of Sicily.

Bradley then moved to London, taking command of the United States ground forces preparing to invade France, commanding First US Army during Operation *Overlord* and the subsequent battle for Normandy. He took command of the new 12th Army Group in July and led it across France to the German border where it fought difficult battles along the Siegfried Line. Bradley's command would eventually become the largest United States Army field command in history with over one million soldiers.

## Field Marshal Bernard L. Montgomery (1887–1976), commander of 21st Army Group

Montgomery commanded 3rd Division during the German invasion of the Low Countries in May 1940, guiding it back to Dunkirk so it could be evacuated to England. He then commanded II Corps, V Corps and XII Corps before taking over South-East Command in December 1941.

Following the sudden death of Eighth Army's commander, Montgomery found himself facing Field Marshal Erwin Rommel's Africa Korps in Egypt, North Africa, in August 1942. After consolidating his position his troops attacked at El Alamein in October, driving the Axis out of Egypt and Libya, back into Tunisia. He continued in command of Eighth Army during the battle for Tunisia and the invasions of Sicily and Italy.

Montgomery moved to England at the end of 1943, taking command of 21st Army Group and all ground troops preparing for Operation *Overlord*. He commanded the Army Group during the difficult battle for Normandy, the advance into Belgium and the failed Operation *Market Garden*. Eisenhower gave Montgomery command of the northern half of the Ardennes battlefield when it became too difficult for Bradley to control it all.

# The US Army Commanders

Two US Armies were engaged during the Battle of the Ardennes and their commanders were two different characters. First Army held the original Ardennes front but would eventually fall back to hold the northern shoulder as Army Group B advanced. Third Army would take over the southern shoulder and make the initial counterattack. While General Hodges was a calm and solid soldier, General Patton was flamboyant and erratic; both were professional soldiers who got the job done.

General Courtney H. Hodges (1887–1966) served as Chief of Infantry and commander of the Replacement and School Command before taking over X Corps in May 1942. He was promoted to Third Army in February 1943 and accompanied it to England in January 1944, where he became Bradley's deputy at First Army, taking responsibility for training. He served as Bradley's eyes and ears during the Normandy campaign and was promoted to command First Army at the end of July.

General George S. Patton Jr. (1885–1945), was promoted from 2nd Armored Division to command I Armored Corps immediately after Pearl Harbor in December 1941. He served briefly as II Corps' commander in Tunisia, North Africa, in the spring of 1943, earning the nickname 'Blood and Guts', before returning to I Armored Corps. His command was renamed Seventh Army in July 1943, but at the end of the Sicily campaign he hit the headlines for slapping a convalescing soldier. Patton moved to England early in 1944 as commander of the fictional First US Army Group (FUSAG), which was invented to mislead the Germans into believing that the Allies intend to invade France by way of Calais. He narrowly escaped dismissal after making inflammatory comments in front of a member of the press but was promoted to command Third Army in Normandy at the end of July.

## Army Group B's Final Planning

The instructions issued to Rundstedt and Model on 19 October called for three armies advancing side-by-side through the Belgian Ardennes on a 65-mile-wide front. Sixth Panzer Army would be on the right (or north) flank of the attack, Fifth Panzer Army was in the centre and Seventh Army would protect the left flank as they turned northeast towards Antwerp. Fifteenth Army would extend the attack northwards once it was underway. Ten army corps with ten mechanized (panzer or panzer grenadier) and eighteen infantry divisions would lead the assault; they were supported by nine artillery corps and seven *Werfer* brigades. There would be four panzer divisions in the first wave, six in the second wave and three more would join later on. Fifteenth Army would add one mechanized and five infantry divisions.

While the three Armies were preparing to assemble behind Army Group B's line in the Ardennes, Rundstedt was worried that the Allies could break through elsewhere. Although he wanted to reinforce threatened sectors of his line, the opposite was happening as divisions were being stripped from the line so they could prepare for the offensive. On 5 November Hitler ordered Rundstedt to hold the line with what he had and made it clear that divisions committed to the offensive could not be moved without his permission.

Rundstedt was expecting an Allied attack and he believed that Hitler might abandon his plans if they did. When Third US Army attacked near Metz on 8 November he was still not allowed to use the divisions earmarked for *Wacht am Rhein* and was reduced to falsifying the commitment of divisions to stop the Americans breaking through. A second attack, at Aachen, starting on 16 November, mauled several divisions earmarked for the Ardennes and used up valuable ammunition and fuel. When it was clear that it was pointless arguing any more with the Führer, Rundstedt went ahead with planning for the Big Solution.

By the end of November Hitler's plans were falling into place. On paper Army Group B's Order of Battle looked impressive;

Model issued a final warning in mid November: 'Should the attack be stopped at the Meuse due to the lack of reserves, the only result will be a bulge in the line and not the destruction of sizable enemy forces … The widely stretched flanks, especially in the south, will only invite enemy counteractions.' His predictions would turn out to be remarkably accurate.

the problem was it was founded on falsehoods and half-truths. While field commanders submitted accurate unit sizes and supply estimates, Jodl altered them to match Hitler's plans. Distortions were then repeated until they were taken as fact, resulting in fictional figures being factored into the operational planning. Problems would only surface when units were ordered into battle and found to be far smaller than anticipated or short of equipment and transport; or even worse, they did not exist.

## Operation *Wacht am Rhein*: Army Group B Order of Battle and Objectives

*Oberbefehlshaber West; Generalfeldmarschall Gerd von Rundstedt*
*Army Group B; Generalfeldmarschall Walter Model*

### Sixth Panzer Army;
### Oberstgruppenführer der Waffen SS Josef Dietrich

North Flank: LXVII Corps; Generalleutnant Otto Hitzfeld
South Flank: I SS Panzer Corps; SS-Gruppenführer Hermann Priess
Second Wave: II SS Panzer Corps; SS-Obergruppenführer Willi Bittrich

1  Advance through Verviers and Malmédy, parallel with the Amblève River
2  Wheel northwest, crossing the River Meuse at Liège and Huy
3  Advance for Maastricht and Antwerp while Fifteenth Army protected their right flank

*General Joseph 'Sepp' Dietrich.*

Josef 'Sepp' Dietrich (1892–1966) was Hitler's bodyguard before he became commander of the *Leibstandarte SS Adolf Hitler* Regiment and he took part in the murder of Nazi opponents during the Night of the Long Knives in 1934. The Regiment increased to division size on the eve of the Second World War and Dietrich took part in the invasion of France, Greece, Yugoslavia and Russia. He was promoted to command *I SS Panzerkorps* on the Eastern Front but after leading it through the Normandy campaign in the summer of 1944 he was promoted to command Sixth Panzer Army.

## Fifth Panzer Army;
## General der Panzertruppen Hasso von Manteuffel

North Flank: LXVI Corps; General der Artillerie Walter Lucht
Centre: LVIII Panzer Corps; General der Panzertruppen Walter Krüger

Hasso von Manteuffel (1897–1978) taught at the Berlin-Krampnitz Panzer Troop School until he was appointed regimental commander in April 1941 in time for the invasion of Russia. He was promoted to brigade commander in July 1942 and then division commander in North Africa early in 1943. By the summer of 1943 Manteuffel was back in Russia and in September 1944 he was promoted to command Fifth Panzer Army ready for the Ardennes battle.

South Flank: XLVII Panzer Corps; General der Panzertruppen Heinrich Freiherr von Lüttwitz

Second Wave: XXXIX Panzer Corps; Generalleutant Karl Decker

1  Advance through St Vith and Bastogne, crossing the Our, Clerf and Salm Rivers
2  Advance northwest across the Ourthe, Lesse and L'Homme to the Meuse at Namur
3  Establish a line through Antwerp – Brussels – Namur – Dinant

## Seventh Army;
## General der Panzertruppen Erich Brandenberger

North Flank: LXXXV Corps; General der Infantrerie Baptist Kniess
Centre: LXXX Corps; General der Infanterie Franz Beyer
South Flank: LIII Corps; General der Kavallerie Edwin von Rothkirch

1  Cross the River Our and the River Clerf and advance to the south of Bastogne
2  Advance west through Neufchâteau
3  Secure Army Group B's south flank and take Luxembourg City if possible

## The Allied Situation

The Allied situation on the Western Front at the end of November was as follows:

*Brandenberger (left) and Manteuffel.*

Erich Brandenberger (1892–1955) served as XXIII Army Corps' Chief of Staff on the West Wall from September 1939. He was given command of 8th Panzer Division in February 1941 and promoted to LIX Corps in January 1943. Brandenberger joined XXIX Corps on the Eastern Front in November 1943 and in the autumn of 1944 he was promoted to command Seventh Army in time for the Ardennes Offensive.

## 21st Army Group

First Canadian and Second British Army's North of the Waal River in Holland

## 12th Army Group

First and Ninth US Armies: Advancing towards Bonn and Cologne
Third US Army: Along the Saar River

## 6th Army Group

Seventh US Army: Around Strasbourg on the Rhine
First French Army: Containing German forces in the Colmar pocket

On 7 December General Dwight D. Eisenhower, Air Chief Marshal Sir Arthur W. Tedder, Field Marshal Sir Bernard L. Montgomery, and Lieutenant General Omar N. Bradley discussed future strategy at Maastricht. Montgomery supported a single thrust across the Rhine, north of the Ruhr, and Eisenhower allocated Ninth US Army to 21 Army Group for the task. Third US Army was also to prepare for an advance towards Frankfurt while Seventh US Army turned north into the Saverne Gap. Allied casualties had

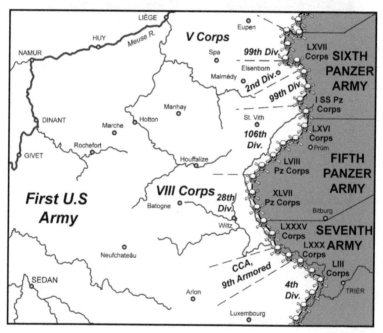

*Detail of Army Group B on O-Tag. While Sixth Panzer and Fifth Panzer Armies would advance in a northwest arc across the River Meuse while Seventh Army covered their exposed southern flank.*

been high in the autumn of 1944 and there was a shortage of replacements.

With new attacks planned, the Allied line had to be thin somewhere and the First US Army sector through the Eifel and Ardennes, with its poor road network and quiet reputation was the ideal choice. VIII Corps had less than 70,000 men holding an 85-mile sector; it was three times the normal length and a gamble the Allies had to take.

## V Corps: Major General Leonard T. Gerow

Holding Monschau and Gerolstein Forests

## VIII Corps: Major General Troy H. Middleton

Holding the Schnee Eifel ridge, the Our and Sauer Rivers

# The Soldiers

## Army Group B

Many soldiers in Army Group B would have worn the field grey (*feldgrau*), Model 1936 tunic. It had four front patch pockets and some were designed so an equipment belt could be fitted to hooks outside of the tunic. Volksturm units were issued with the cheaper Model 1944, a shorter drab greenish-brown tunic with no suspension system. Field grey trousers had tapered ankles to fit into the ankle boots (*Schnürschuhe*) and canvas gaiters (*Gamaschen*).

Black belts and suspenders, or braces, two up the front and one up the back, were used to carry equipment. Ammunition pouches, entrenching tool, knife, bread bag, water bottle and gas mask tin were clipped onto the belt. A soldier carried the rest of his equipment and personal items in the haversack and it was slung on the back, along with the tent piece and mess tin, using an A-frame support.

> None of VIII Corps troops had a high fighting efficiency. 4th and 28th Infantry Division had recently moved to the Ardennes to rest after the Hürtgen Forest battle. 106th Division and 9th Armoured Division had only just arrived on the Continent and had been sent to the Ardennes area to train.

All soldiers wore the coal scuttle helmet and while colour could range from dark black-green to slate-grey to olive-green, many were covered with a variety of factory-made or improvised camouflage covers.

Tank troops wore a short green field jacket with a black side cap or peaked field cap. They also had a one-piece denim overall worn during maintenance duties called a *Panzerkombi*. Trousers had tapered cuffs to fit into lace-up ankle boots.

Waffen SS units wore a variety of clothing because suppliers could not keep up with demand. Most troops wore either the Model 1942–43 with four breast pockets or the shorter Model 44 with only two pockets; both were in grey-green. During shortages troops were issued with standard army uniforms. Some would also wear their mottled camouflage smocks with their tapered cuffs and waist.

All troops were issued with heavy wool greatcoats or hooded waterproof parkas in winter conditions. If possible they were also issued with white over-smocks when it snowed, but men sometimes had to make their own out of sheets. Men often took winter clothing and boots off prisoners and dead GIs because they considered them better quality.

Officers were armed with Walther P38 pistols while the MP40 machine pistol was issued to platoon and squad leaders; the StG44 assault rifle had also just started to be introduced. Other ranks carried the Karabiner 98 Kurz, or Kar98k, bolt action rifle and the stick handle Model 43 grenade (*Stielhandgranate*). Squads relied on the impressive rate of fire of the MG 42 machine gun to provide covering fire.

Infantry units had two types of shoulder-mounted anti-tank weapons and while the Panzerfaust was a lightweight single shot disposable weapon, the Panzershcreck was a heavier, reusable version.

## First and Third Armies

US Army soldiers wore two types of uniforms. Men serving with divisions which had been in Europe for some time wore the older style olive drab herringbone cotton twill (HBT) uniform over a wool service shirt. The single breasted jacket had two breast pockets while the trousers tucked into the leather gaiters which covered the ankle and the top of the combat service boots. Airborne troops and men serving in divisions which reached Europe towards the end of 1944 wore the improved M-1943 olive drab cotton sateen

*An infantry patrol searches the snow-covered woods on V Corps front while Sixth Panzer Army's tanks gather a short distance away. (NARA 111-SC-197350)*

version complete with four-pocket field jacket, detachable jacket hood, and field trousers. All troops had their unit patch and rank on their sleeves.

An anorak style winter combat jacket in olive drab was issued during cold weather and overshoes were worn to reduce the chances of getting trench foot, a debilitating problem caused by prolonged exposure of the feet to wet and cold conditions.

All soldiers wore a fatigue hat or peaked cap while carrying out maintenance duties in the rear areas and a manganese steel pot helmet painted with olive drab paint when they were in the combat zone.

A soldier had to carry a lot of essential equipment at all times and his knife, canteen, first aid pouch and magazine pouches were attached to the belt which was supported by suspenders. The rest of his equipment and personal items were carried in a small olive drab cotton canvas backpack. A few soldiers would have the new two-part back pack with the Combat Field Pack for essential items above the Cargo Field Pack for non-essential items; the Cargo Field Pack could be detached in combat. Soldiers also carried an M1943 entrenching tool with folding shovel which could be strapped to their back in a canvas cover.

Many GIs were equipped with the M1 Garand gas-operated, semi-automatic rifle with an eight-round clip and the 10-inch M1 bayonet. Others, particularly officers, NCOs, artillery observers and airborne troops were issued with the M1 Carbine, a smaller and lighter rifle which used a reduced power cartridge. Officers would also carry the M1911A1 automatic pistol while other ranks carried a number of M2 fragmentation hand grenades.

The main US Army sub machine gun at this time was the M1A1 Thompson submachine gun although a few soldiers would have been issued with the new M3 submachine gun, which was known as the Grease Gun. The squad support weapon was the Browning Automatic Rifle, or BAR, a .30 calibre, gas-operated, air-cooled, automatic rifle. Both the water cooled M1917 and lighter air cooled M1919 Browning heavy machine gun could be mounted on vehicles.

Infantry units used the M1919 with a tripod to provide heavy fire support.

The GI could rely on the M9 Bazooka to take on tanks, although some M1 Bazookas might still have been around. Although they also had the M3A1 anti-tank gun, it was ineffective against most German tanks. Mortars for the infantry came in two sizes, the heavier M2 81mm mortar and the lighter M2 mortar.

*Most of new tanks, like this massive King Tiger, went straight from the factories to the Western Front, ready for Operation Wacht am Rhein. These men of 129th Ordnance Battalion are bringing this captured specimen back for inspection unaware that two panzer armies were assembling behind the German lines. (NARA 111-SC-197752)*

# The Kit

## Army Group B

While Hitler had made sure that Army Group B's panzer divisions were at full strength at the start of the offensive, the ravaged state of the German armaments industry meant that there were few replacements. The main armament of a tank (or panzer, short for panzerkampfwagen, or battle tank) was mounted in a fully rotating turret. The Wehrmacht's philosophy on tank warfare was to keep designing bigger and heavier tanks with a larger main armament and thicker armour. They were also slower and unable to use smaller bridges.

While panzer divisions were equipped with a mixture of designs by December 1944 the workhorse was the Panzer IV. Armoured regiments were also equipped with the Panzer V, Panther tank, and the Panzer VI, Tiger I tank. The SS panzer divisions were also equipped with the massive Tiger II, King Tiger tank.

| Mark | Weight/ Main Gun | Max-Min Armour | Road/Cross Country |
|------|------------------|----------------|---------------------|
| Panzer VI, Tiger II | 70 tons 88mm/L71 | 180–80mm | 30–15 km/hr |
| Panzer VI, Tiger I | 57 tons 88mm/L56 | 100–80mm armour | 38–15 km/hr |
| Panzer V, Panther | 45.5 tons 75mm/L70 | 110–40mm armour | 46–30 km/hr |
| Panzer IV | 23 tons 75mm/L48 | 50–30mm armour | 40–16 km/hr |

German 'tank hunters' had low silhouettes and their crews used stealth and cover to track down enemy tanks. There were three types armed with fixed 75mm/L48 guns mounted on top of tank hulls. The Sturmgeschütz IV was based on a Panzer IV, the Stug III was built on a Panzer III and the Hetzer was based on a Panzer

38(t). Infantry units used the 7.5cm PaK 40 anti-tank gun and the formidable 8.8cm FlaK gun to fight off enemy armour.

Over 1,900 artillery pieces supported Army Group B's opening attack and they ranged from the light 75mm guns supporting the infantry to huge 210mm heavy guns. There were also large numbers of 15cm and 21cm Nebelwerfers, terrifying multiple rocket launchers. While Volksgrenadier units used a mixture of halftracks, lorries and horses to move their artillery, panzer divisions were supported by two types of self-propelled artillery. The Nashorn was armed with an 88mm/L71 while the Hummel had a 150mm/L30 gun.

Panzer grenadiers used the Sdkfz 251 halftrack to move across the battlefield. Variants mounted a range of items including mortars, anti-tank guns and radio systems. Armoured reconnaissance units deployed a variety of fast moving four- and eight-wheeled armoured cars to scout ahead of the advance.

## First and Third Army

While the Germans kept making bigger and heavy tanks, the US Army stuck with the same two designs. The smaller M5A1 Stuart only carried a 37mm gun and had armour ranging from 64mm to 29mm. At only 15.5 tons it could travel up to 58 km/hr and was useful for probing enemy positions along with the eight-wheeled Greyhound armoured car.

The main battle tank of the US Army was the M4A3 Sherman (and its variations) which carried a 75mm gun and had armour ranging from 51mm to 38mm. It weighed 31.6 tons, and could travel at up to 32 km/hr. While the Sherman was out-gunned by the German designs, the standard design made maintenance easier.

The US Army used three types of tank destroyers, all with rotating turrets, to hunt down enemy tanks and the M18 Hellcat was the light and fast version. The M10 tank destroyer was armed with a 76.2mm gun while the M36 Jackson armed was with the 90mm gun.

US Army armored infantry rode in the M3 halftrack. Variants of the halftracks mounted a range of items including mortars, anti-tank guns and radio systems. The M3 based Multiple Gun Motor Carriage anti-aircraft variant, armed with Quad 50, was used as a deadly infantry support weapon.

The 57mm anti-tank gun was unable to penetrate the armour of most German tanks while the M2 90mm gun was easy to spot. In many cases the infantry relied on mines to immobilize a tank and M9 bazookas to knock them out.

Infantry units were supported by M2 105mm, the M1 155mm, and the 155mm Long Tom howitzers while airborne divisions were armed with the M1 75mm and M3 105mm howitzers. Armoured divisions were equipped with the self propelled M7 Priest, armed with a 105mm howitzer. The M8 Howitzer Motor Carriage, armed with a 75mm, had mainly been replaced by a Sherman-based variant armed with a 105mm howitzer.

# The Tactics

## Army Group B

The whole emphasis during Army Group B's advance was to advance as fast as possible to the capture the bridges across the River Meuse. The plan was for the Volks Grenadier Divisions to overrun First US Army's outposts and clear the way for the panzer divisions. Once the armour was moving, the Volks Grenadier troops could regroup and mop up behind them, securing lines of communication for the armour.

Panzer divisions were organised into kampfgruppes, or battle groups, consisting of a mixture of panzers, panzer grenadiers and self propelled artillery, and the emphasis was on speed. Success depended on them advancing deep into enemy territory, avoiding enemy concentrations of troops unless absolutely necessary. However, in the Ardennes the road network was limited and the panzer kampfgruppes had little room for manoeuvre due to the difficult terrain and the muddy nature of the ground. Allied air superiority over the Ardennes meant that while US armour could move where it wanted in clear weather, German armour had to watch out for the Allied fighter bombers.

Reconnaissance units led the way, looking to spring ambushes, find unguarded detours and spot targets for the artillery. They would keep the kampfgruppes up to date on the enemy positions so that a plan of attack could be made. When possible the kampfgruppe commander would aim to bypass a centre of resistance or roadblock, however, in many cases there was no option but to bludgeon a way through.

Panzer grenadiers would drive through small arms fire to get to their objective, while avoiding concentrations of artillery fire. The heavy machine guns mounted on their halftracks would keep the enemy's heads down until it was too late, while tanks provided supporting fire.

## First and Third Armies

During the early stages of Army Group B's attack there was no time for tactics, all the men at the front could do was to hold on as long as possible, blocking as many roads as possible to delay the German advance. There was a tendency to hold onto villages, particularly those on watercourses, because they were natural bottlenecks in the German advance. On several occasions German tank columns saw the bridge they needed being demolished, resulting in a delay while the engineers made repairs.

The only way Army Group B could be stopped was to delay the armoured columns. Corps reserves and engineers were despatched to key points on the road network. While some of the engineers prepared bridges for demolition the rest organised the building of roadblocks. A variety of traps were laid for the German panzers but the favourites were to lay mines in the road or to use explosive charges to bring down trees to block them. At the same time slit trenches and gun positions would be dug to cover the roadblock, and stragglers were expected to man them rather than falling back to the rear. Troops would have orders only to open fire when the German engineers were clearing the obstruction. Each delay would give more time for new roadblocks to be built.

The plan was to send reinforcements to defend key towns behind First US Army's front. Towns stood at key road junctions, and Army Group B would be forced to use side roads to keep moving if they could not take them. Troops were often formed into small combat teams or task forces, composed of infantry and armour, and sent to hold a village or road junction for as long as possible. This gave larger combat teams time to form a tight perimeter around the outskirts of a town.

Armoured divisions had two active combat commands with a third in reserve. Reconnaissance armoured cars and jeeps went ahead to scout the enemy positions and spring ambushes. Each combat command had a mixture of tanks and armoured infantry units, usually travelling together in columns along roads with tanks and halftracks loaded with infantry mixed together. The infantry would dismount and engage the enemy if the ground was soft, while the tanks and halftracks gave covering fire from the road. Vehicles would only leave a road if they were absolutely sure that the ground was hard enough to travel across without getting bogged down.

During Third Army's offensive General Patton wanted his armour to advance as quickly as possible, driving deep into German-held territory while the armoured infantry mopped up the villages behind. The Germans also resorted to using roadblocks and demolishing bridges to stall Third Army. The extreme weather meant troops tended to seek shelter in villages, a dangerous move because artillery could easily target their billets while armour moved in for the kill.

# THE DAYS BEFORE BATTLE

## Deceiving the Allies

One of Hitler's main provisos during the initial discussions was for absolute secrecy. He only involved Rundstedt, Model and a handful of senior staff officers in the final planning and everyone was sworn to secrecy on pain of death. While notes were recorded in separate war diaries, all communications were monitored while correspondence was carried by trusted liaison officers who were watched at all times. Secrecy was maintained through a combination of stern authority and absolute obedience.

While the Ardennes was the Allies' weakest sector, it could easily be reinforced if news or even rumours of an attack got out. The Wehrmacht had to make SHAEF look elsewhere and the scenario that OB West used was that it was expecting a breakthrough between Cologne and Bonn. Sixth Panzer Army remained in the area with four armoured divisions as a large counterattack force. Towards the end of November a temporary Twenty-Fifth Army was created in the Eifel area as part of the deception.

Army Group B's concentration area ranged from the Moselle River in the south and the Rhine in the east. Troops north of Mönchengladbach and Roermond assembled as normal to draw

*Eisenhower meets General Middleton in St Vith in November, not realising that the town would later become a focal point of the battle.*

Allied attention to them, but maximum concealment was used in the area Bonn, Euskirchen and Monschau. While radio traffic focused American eyes on the concentration of German armour east of Aachen, any movements in the Eifel region were carried out in utmost secrecy. The cover plan was so effective that it fooled the German commanders as much as their American counterparts.

The US Air Force had air superiority on the Western Front, but the Ardennes and Eifel areas were low on their list of priorities. Even so the German troops had to be camouflage experts and they spent daylight hours hiding in forests and villages, only daring to move at night. Patrolling was limited on the front line to limit the chances of prisoners being taken, radio blackouts were ordered and no pre-artillery registration was allowed. While thousands of German troops and hundreds of vehicles converged on the Eifel area the big question was, would the Allied planes spot them?

By December 1944 12th Army Group believed that the Germans lacked the manpower, armour, planes, ammunition and fuel needed to attack. On the 12th its diary reported; 'It is now certain that attrition is steadily sapping the strength of German forces on the Western Front and that the crust of defences is thinner, more brittle and more vulnerable than it appears on our G-2 maps or to the troops in the line.' Rundstedt's return had been noted and it was expected that he would counterattack and then withdraw behind the Rhine. It was believed that the German armoured reserve would be used to stop the attack in the Roer area and while Sixth Panzer Army was thought to be in the Cologne area, it was believed that Fifth Panzer Army was in command of resting divisions.

By mid December SHAEF intelligence had only identified seven of the 28 divisions earmarked for the offensive. Occasional reports of increased vehicle activity at night were dismissed as rumours while a report that woods near Bitburg were full of vehicles did not reach First US Army headquarters until it was too late. Four prisoners were taken on 15 December but their vague stories of an imminent attack were also dismissed.

Poor weather continued to limit air intelligence over the Ardennes and intermittent reports of troop movements west of the Rhine were attributed to reinforcements moving north and south to stop First and Third US Armies.

## Assembling for Battle

On 10 November Hitler set 25 November as the date to attack. It was chosen because of poor flying weather but it could not be met for four reasons:

1   Divisions were still tied up at Aachen and Metz and needed time to replace casualties
2   The Replacement Army needed extra time to train the Volks Grenadier divisions
3   A shortage of fuel was delaying armour and transport getting to the assembly areas
4   More time was needed to stockpile ammunition and fuel

Once the offensive had been delayed until mid-December, the question was would the bad weather hold?

In the three-month period before the attack around the area east of the Ardennes was a hive of secret activity. As well as the mass of men, vehicles and armour moving into the concentration area, 2,000 trains delivered nearly 150,000 tons of supplies. The two panzer armies took over the rail lines on 10 December and careful control of train movements allowed hundreds of tanks and other heavy equipment to be moved and unloaded during the hours of darkness or bad flying weather. Although there were air attacks on the railway network, the Allies preferred to attack industries.

100 trains also delivered over 15,000 tons of ammunition. It was far lower than Army Group B asked for because estimates were based on achieving a rapid breakthrough with limited fighting. However, the big supply problem was fuel; half of the 4.5 million gallons collected for the offensive were still stockpiled in depots along the Rhine.

During the final planning stage, Hitler decided to add a commando style aspect to 1st SS Panzer Division's advance. Operation Greif (or Condor) involved soldiers wearing GI uniforms and riding in captured American vehicles. Disguised raiding parties would drive through V Corps lines and capture one or two Meuse bridges while an armoured brigade followed; sabotage parties would create confusion behind the American lines. Rumours that the raiders were planning to assassinate Allied leaders, notably General Eisenhower, were later dismissed.

Lieutenant Colonel Otto Skorzeny had a reputation as a resourceful leader, having rescued Mussolini and then seized the Hungarian Regent in daring operations. Panzer Brigade 150 (or Brandenburger Brigade) numbered 2,000 men, some of them English speaking, and they were dressed in captured uniforms and given false identification papers. They were equipped with a mixture of captured and modified tanks, halftracks and vehicles.

On 26 November Jodl told Rundstedt that Null Tag (D-day) was set for 10 December. It was delayed again to the 16th to give

At the last minute an airborne element was added to Sixth Panzer Army's attack and Col. Friedrich von der Heydte was only given eight days to organize a 1,000 parachute unit. Troops would parachute into the Elsenborn-Malmédy area, seizing roads ahead of 1st SS Panzer Division.

troops time to get into position and to deliver fuel to the front line depots. At the end of the first week in December corps and division commanders were told about their objectives and they in turn briefed their staffs on 10 December. Hitler then spoke to all his commanders on the nights of 11 and 12 December. Divisions could then start gathering in their assembly areas:

Infantry   Area I six miles and Area II three miles behind the front
Armour   Area I twelve miles and Area II: six to ten miles behind
the front

Seventh Army then had to handover its positions to the incoming units without arousing suspicion. The final movement dates were scheduled as follows:

| | |
|---|---|
| 12 December | K-Tag: Troops alerted for movement |
| 13 December | L-Tag: Infantry into Area I, rocket launchers and horse drawn artillery in place |
| 14 December | M-Tag: Infantry and armour into Area II, motorized artillery into position |
| 15 December | N-Tag: All formations to the line of departure or forward combat positions |
| 16 December | O-Tag: Attack! |

All movements were made at night while the Luftwaffe flew overhead to drown out the noise of moving vehicles. The troops were eventually told what their objectives were on the night of the

*Panther tanks being delivered to Sixth Panzer Army by rail.*

15th and everyone was in place an hour or two before H-hour, 05:30 hours on the morning of 16 December.

Army Group B had assembled a formidable force, one larger than the Allies thought possible, but more importantly, it was assembled in secret where the American's least expected an attack. The final composition of the attack was as follows:

Thirteen infantry and seven armoured divisions in the first wave
Five divisions, one armoured and one mechanized brigade in the second wave
Five divisions and 450 tanks armoured assault guns in OKW reserve
1,900 artillery pieces and rocket projectors
970 tanks and armoured assault guns

Fifteenth Army would join the north flank of the attack later on, increasing the number to 29 infantry divisions and twelve mechanised divisions. Göring had also promised 1,000 planes but few doubted that it was more than a promise.

While the numbers looked impressive on paper, there were many problems at lower levels of command. As noted earlier Jodl had altered unit strength assessments to suit Hitler's plans. The number of available artillery pieces was also lower than expected because of shortage of transport and fuel; most units would suffer from a scarcity of both items.

There were also deficiencies of support weapons while a lot of signal and engineering equipment was out of date. It did not take a military expert to work out that the offensive had been planned on a shoestring. The question was, would the shoestring hold or snap?

On 15 December Model asked Rundstedt to postpone the attack; he refused. O-Tag would go ahead as planned and at midnight the following entry was made in OB West's War Diary: 'Tomorrow brings the beginning of a new chapter in the Campaign in the West.' What would be the ending of that chapter?

What Hitler must have dreamed of on a massive scale. As 1st SS Panzer Division breaks free and heads west, a King Tiger rolls forward past a line of American prisoners heading into captivity.

# THE GERMAN OFFENSIVE

## 16–17 December
## Operation *Wacht am Rhein* Begins

### Sixth Panzer Army's Frustrating Breakthrough

Dietrich's plan was for LXVII Corps to establish a protective flank at Monschau on Sixth Panzer Army's north flank, while I SS Panzer Corps advanced west across the Hohes Venn. Three Volks Grenadier divisions would break through First US Army's line and turn north to block the roads from Verviers. Three panzer divisions would then pass through the gap and head west towards Malmédy; II SS Panzer Corps' two panzer divisions would follow.

99th Division faced I SS Panzer Corps and having just arrived on the Continent, it was cooperating with 2nd Division in V Corps attacks against the West Wall to gain experience. A build up of German units had been noted but General Middleton assumed they had gathered to counterattack. 14th Cavalry Group held the Our River valley in VIII Corps sector, facing Sixth Panzer Army's south flank.

A devastating 90-minute barrage by two artillery corps and several rocket launcher brigades isolated many of 99th Division's

Army Group B's timetable had the Volks Grenadiers breaking through on day one, the armour passing through on day two and crossing the Meuse on day four. While the barrage began at 05:30am on 16 December on large parts of Army Group B's front, the infantry would infiltrate the American lines in silence on others.

*Men of the 2nd Division hug the sides of a shallow ditch as German shells rain down on their positions on Elsenborn Ridge. Over-stretched and undermanned, First US Army's weak line had little chance of holding back Army Group B's attack. (NARA 111-SC-197304)*

front line units and cut communications to the rear. The dazed GIs emerged from their dugouts to find Volks Grenadier troops advancing through the forests and a confused battle for survival followed. Sixth Panzer Army's advance through the mist was delayed by a combination of heavy resistance and minefields, throwing Dietrich's timetable into disarray.

In LXVII Corps sector 326th VG Division's attack was stopped in its tracks around Monschau while in I SS Panzer Corps' sector 277th VG Division only made slow progress towards the twin villages of Rocherath and Krinkelt. 12th SS Panzer Division eventually had to send tanks forward to help the Volks Grenadiers' advance. While 12th VG Division initially made progress, surprising US troops queuing for breakfast at Buchholz station, its advance was stopped at Losheimergraben. 12th SS Panzer Division again had to send tanks forward to help but they too were stopped at Hünningen.

I SS Panzer Corps' only real success came after 12th VG Division cleared 14th Cavalry Group from Lanzerath on Sixth Panzer Army's right flank. It allowed 3d Parachute Division to advance through the Losheim Gap in the afternoon and move around 2nd Division's flank. The demolition of the Losheim railway bridge meant that 1st SS Panzer Division's planned route was blocked, so Dietrich ordered it to exploit the gap at Lanzerath, turning north to rejoin its allotted route at Buchholz.

By nightfall 99th Division was still holding most of its original line but all its reserves had been committed. While V Corps had a few reinforcements to send forward, Sixth Panzer Army had still to commit its four SS panzer divisions.

On 17 December, 99th Division withdrew and while 393rd Regiment dug in around Rocherath, 395th Regiment did the same at Krinkelt. 277th VG Division and 12th SS Panzer Division followed close behind and the start of a prolonged and bitter fight for the twin villages began. The dogged defence allowed 2nd Division to withdraw from its exposed salient and move south through the villages to take up positions around Wirtzfeld.

Sergeant Vernon McGarity, 393rd Regt, 99th Division, fought on behind enemy lines around Krinkelt despite being wounded, knocking out a tank and a machine gun team single-handed. Pfc. William A. Soderman, 9th Rgt, 2nd Division, drove off armoured attacks around Rocherath with his bazooka and was seriously wounded. Both men were awarded the Medal of Honor.

> The parachute drop on the Hohes Venn was delayed until the morning of 17 December. Bad winds scattered the paratroopers and Heydte only found 300 stragglers. By the 21st it was clear I SS Panzer Corps would not reach them and they tried to escape.

394th Regiment held onto Murringen until it was surrounded on the evening of the 17th; the men escaped on foot. They were not the only ones; around 850 men, many of them wounded, made it back from other parts of 99th Division's front line positions, slipping though the German lines to reach Elsenborn.

1st SS Panzer Regiment cleared Buchholz during the night of the 16th/17th and then continued its advance through Honsfeld, destroying a column of escaping American vehicles. After hearing that the allotted road to Schoppen was virtually impassable, *Obersturmbannführer* Joachim Peiper ordered his Kampfgruppe north into Büllingen, finding a large fuel dump. After refuelling, it turned southwest back onto its allotted route.

Although Peiper had broken through the American lines, the inflexibility of Sixth Panzer Army's plan would cost it dearly. Had the Kampfgruppe turned north it would have taken Krinkelt and Rocherath in the rear, allowing the rest of I SS Panzer Corps to advance. 99th Division's commander, Major General Walter E. Lauer later commented; 'The enemy had the key to success within his hands, but did not know it.' As Peiper's advance guard moved to the south of Malmédy it ran into a US Army convoy belonging to Battery B of the 285th Field Artillery Observation Battalion at Baugnez crossroads. After shooting up the trucks and placing around 100 soldiers under guard, it continued west into Ligneuville. Two hours later the prisoners were marched into a roadside field and executed; only a handful escaped by feigning death.

On the afternoon of 17 December Peiper's advance guard drove into Stavelot and attacked the US troops guarding the bridge over the

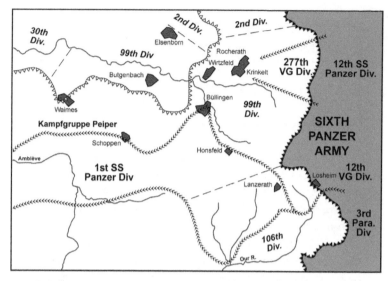

*Sixth Panzer Army's advance, 16/17 December. Once Kampfgruppe Peiper broke through the Losheim Gap, it was free to advance quickly west along the Amblève valley. By the time Rocherath and Krinkelt were taken, Sixth Panzer Army faced V Corps' strong position around Elsenborn.*

*The aftermath of Peiper's 'wave of terror and fright' at Baugnez Crossroads; bodies left by the roadside in the snow. (NARA 111-SC-200346)*

Baugnez was not the first massacre in I SS Panzer Corps' area, there had been others at Honsfeld and Büllingen, and it would not be the last. They were carried out under the order to create a 'wave of terror and fright' and by the end of the battle over 350 soldiers and 100 civilians had been executed. News of the massacre spread quickly and if anything, it made the American soldiers more determined to fight.

Amblève. They withdrew as night fell, not realising than only a single engineer squad was standing in its way. Peiper had already travelled 20 miles since the attack began, making the sort of advance Dietrich expected; but it was Sixth Panzer Army's only success.

During the night there was confusion on both sides of the river. On the south bank a radio failure meant that Peiper did not know that 12th SS Panzer Division had still not moved. Across the valley the road to Malmédy was nose to tail with US Army vehicles trying to escape and many of the trucks had been ordered to clear the gasoline dumps north of Stavelot and Malmédy.

## Fifth Panzer Army's Attack has Mixed Results

General Middleton's VIII Corps held the Schnee Eifel, a heavily forested ridge, in front of LXVI Corps. It was a vulnerable position, with the River Our to its rear and few roads running west. Part of the West Wall fortifications ran along the crest of the ridge and First US Army did not want to give up the position. 106th Division held the ridge and it was new to the Continent, having been only been in the front line for a few days. While the soldiers held many pillboxes, they were inexperienced and suffering from a shortage of mines and automatic weapons. 14th Cavalry Group held the Our Valley on the division's north flank.

General Manteuffel wanted LXVI Corps to make a pincer attack around the ends of the Schnee Eiffel, meeting up at Schönberg

*The speed of the German advance often took American rear area units by surprise. Though high hopes for Skorzeny's disguised Jeep parties were soon dashed. A few caused some confusion behind V Corps lines but were quickly rounded up, some to be executed as spies.*

before heading west towards St Vith. There was no artillery barrage and 18th VG Division took advantage of the morning mist to infiltrate 14th Cavalry Group's positions in the Losheim Gap north of the Schnee Eifel. By noon it past 106th Division's north flank and attacking artillery positions around Auw. 62nd VG Division failed to take Heckhuscheid, but it forced 424th Regiment back through Winterspelt, exposing 106th Division's south flank. LXVI Corps' pincer attack on the Schnee Eifel was working and while 422nd and 423rd Regiments only faced a thin screen of German troops on the crest of the ridge, their flanks were dangerously exposed.

By nightfall 106th Division was in a dangerous salient and it had already exhausted its reserves. While VIII Corps had ordered two armored combat commands to St Vith, they were too far away to help and Middleton warned General Alan W. Jones about the developing situation. While Middleton suggested withdrawing, he left the decision with 'the man on the ground'. Jones decided to hold on ...

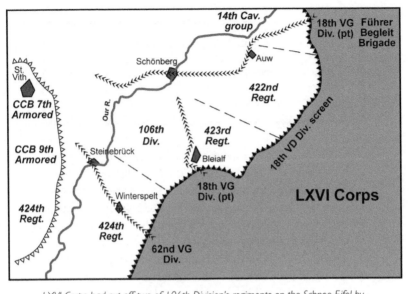

*LXVI Corps had cut off two of 106th Division's regiments on the Schnee Eifel by 17 December, before turning west to attack St Vith.*

At dawn on 17 December, 18th VG Division crossed the River Our at Andler and reached Schönberg by mid morning; cutting the main escape route from the Schnee Eifel. Meanwhile, Lieutenant Jarrett M. Huddleston's small garrison stopped 62nd VG Division taking Steinebrück until CCB, 9th Armored Division arrived.

Plans to advance towards the Schnee Eiffel were shelved and the armour secured the east bank of the Our until 424th Regiment escaped across the river under cover of darkness. While one of 106th Division's regiments was safe, the remaining two were surrounded and all they could do was to dig in and wait for reinforcements. Although they only had limited ammunition, food and medical supplies, arrangements were being made to air drop more.

To the south of 106th Division, 28th Division held a thin line along the River Our and while 112th Regiment faced LVIII Panzer Corps, 110th Regiment faced XLVII Panzer Corps (109th Regiment faced Seventh Army). LVIII Panzer Corps did not use a covering barrage

> Although 28th Infantry Division had been sent to the Ardennes area to rest after heavy fighting in the battle for Hürtgen Forest, General Cota's men were about to be tested for a second time. The division would again live up to its nickname, 'The Bloody Bucket'.

but surprise was not achieved and the advance stalled. 116th Panzer Division could not advance across the boggy ground north of Lutzkampen and precious time was wasted directing it to the corps' southern flank. 560th VG Division also failed to capture the bridge at Sevenig while the Kalborn bridge was demolished; it took all day and night to install a new bridge across the Our.

Although LVIII Panzer Corps had made little progress, German troops were behind both of 112th Regiment's flanks. 116th Panzer Division crossed the Our at Kalborn on 17 December, losing nearly its half of its tanks clearing the west bank of American troops. The surviving tanks could only crawl forward along poor roads and 112th Regiment held the west bank of the Our until nightfall.

26th VG Division crossed the Our in boats and attacked 110th Regiment's positions on the ridge known as Skyline Drive. Major General Norman D. Cota gave the order to hold every position *'at all costs'* and while the infantry battle on the heights intensified, German engineers built bridges across the river so XLVII Panzer Corps' two panzer divisions could cross. 2nd Panzer Division crossed at Dasburg during the night but Colonel Hurley E. Fuller's men delayed its advance through Manarch before stopping it at Clerf. Panzer Lehr Division crossed at Gemünd but the gallant defence of Consthum and Hosingen delayed it.

When Lüttwitz's armour began to approach the River Clerf, Cota ordered his troops to fall back to Clerf and Wiltz to block the roads to Bastogne, a vital road hub in the Ardennes. However, 110th Regiment had been virtually destroyed by XLVII Panzer Corps after two days of ferocious fighting.

*Allied air superiority was a constant source of worry for the German commanders. If the bad weather broke the sky would be full of American fighters and bombers. German guards and their prisoners scan the skies for signs of aircraft.*

## Seventh Army Advances across the Our and Sauer Rivers

General Brandenberger's Seventh Army had many objectives but it only had the four infantry divisions of LXXX and LXXXV Corps and they were stretched out along a thirty-mile-long front. LXXXV Corps faced part of 28th Division on the Army's north flank and it had to use boats and rafts to cross the River Our. 5th Parachute Division quickly crossed the river and infiltrated 109th Regiment's outposts but while the right flank advanced to Hoscheid, just short of the River Clerf, the left flank was stopped at Führen. It took until late on the 17th before engineers installed a bridge at Roth and only then could the corps' assault guns cross and help force a crossing of the Clerf at Kautenbach.

352nd VG Division crossed the river around Gentingen but the right flank was stopped at Longsdorf and Tandel while the left was pinned down along the river bank. Progress towards Ettelbrück

> The Our River caused many problems for Seventh Army. While the infantry crossed quickly in boats and rafts, in many cases it took the engineers far too long to install bridges for armour and artillery to cross. This left the infantry to fight on alone and Seventh Army's advance suffered as a result. When the Americans went on the counterattack their artillery were able to target the congested crossings.

and the River Sauer was then severely hampered by a shortage of armour.

LXXX Corps' attacked on Seventh Army's south flank with 276th VG Division on the right and 212th VG Division on the left. 276th VG Division faced an armoured infantry battalion of 9th Armored Division which had moved to the River Sauer sector to learn about combat; the GIs did not have to wait long before their lesson began. Fog along the river interfered with the artillery barrage and then delayed the infantry crossing the river. By the time the attack got underway 60th Armored Infantry Battalion was alerted and waiting for 276th VG Division.

The infiltration of Schwarz Erntz Ravine allowed the German reserves to capture Müllerthal and move behind the American right flank, breaking the deadlock on the Sauer heights. Major General John W. Leonard gave the order to withdraw on 17 December but while some of his armoured infantry fell back, many outposts found themselves cut off and they opted to fight on. Once again it took time to get a bridge across the river at Wallendorf and the lack of armour stalled 276th VG Division's advance. Brandenberger was planning to sack the divisional commander for lack of progress but he was killed in action before he could do so.

212th VG Division faced 4th Division's 12th Regiment across the Sauer and the *Volksgrenadiers* crossed the river, infiltrating the American outposts either side of Echternach. While good progress was made in the centre, the garrisons in Berdorf and Osweiler held out, limiting the advance. When the only bridge in the division's

*Soldiers occupy a shallow front line position while a Sherman tank covers the forest trail in the distance. (NARA 111-SC-198177)*

sector was destroyed, it became difficult to get ammunition forward or evacuate casualties and morale plummeted.

On 17 December, promises that part of the 10th Armored Division was moving up boosted American morale, while the main threat from Schwarz Erntz Ravine was halted when 9th Armored Division's reserves counterattacked. Major General O. Raymond Barton also deployed 4th Division's reserves in combined infantry-tank teams and they delayed 212th VG Division until nightfall. LXXX Corps' breakthrough came during the night when troops bypassed Osweiler and advanced towards Scheidgen, opening a hole in the centre of 12th Regiment's front.

While American reinforcements were moving forward to counter Seventh Army's advance, Brandenberger was not expecting any more reserves, he would have to fight on with what he had because OKW B and Army Group B were focused on the situation around St Vith and Bastogne.

# 18–19 December
# Army Group B's Breakthrough Begins

## The American Reaction to the Attack

Eisenhower and Bradley were in conference in Paris when they heard news of the German attack. After discussing strategies and making arrangements for reinforcements, Bradley left for 12th Army Group headquarters. They agreed that First US Army needed to hold both sides of the developing salient at all costs, limiting the width of Army Group B's breakthrough. V Corps would hold on in the north and VIII Corps in the south while reinforcements strengthened the shoulders of the salient. The strategy would hopefully force Army Group B's armies into a narrowing corridor as they headed west. Once the advance ran out of momentum, Allied reinforcements could counterattack the base of the corridor and threaten Army Group B's lines of communications. Could enough reinforcements be found and would they reach the battlefield in time?

News of the attack on 16 December was vague but First US Army's initial assessment that Army Group B was trying to restore lost sections of the West Wall soon changed. While the German advance initially seemed to be directed northwest towards Liège, by noon on 17 December observation planes reported that large armoured columns were moving west. Prisoners also confirmed that Sixth Panzer, Fifth Panzer and Seventh Armies had been committed and that the two panzer armies were heading for several locations along the Meuse. But as VIII Corps front line crumbled, communications with the front line became increasingly difficult and news of Army Group B's progress became increasingly sketchy. The lack of information meant that SHAEF found it hard to track the offensive's progress, making it difficult to organise an effective plan of action.

SHAEF's own reserve was limited to 82nd and 101st Airborne Divisions but Eisenhower also promised 10th Armored Division from Third US Army to the south and 7th Armored Division from Ninth US Army to the north; General William Simpson also offered 30th Division and 5th Armored Division from Ninth US Army reserve. 11th Armored Division, 66th and 75th Divisions had just reached the Continent and they were only a few days from the battlefield. Although they had no combat experience, they were at full strength unlike the battle weary divisions at the front. 17th Airborne and 8th Armored Division were also training in the United Kingdom. On 17 December Bradley ordered General Patton to send two extra divisions north from Third US Army, bringing the number of men moving towards First US Army to over 60,000; far more would follow over the next two weeks.

The speed of the German advance meant that the time lag between intelligence reports being made and reserves arriving on the battlefield often resulted in last-minute change to plans. As reinforcements moved forward and stragglers fell back, the traffic jams increased. They were aggravated by the wintry Ardennes weather.

VIII Corps' three infantry divisions had borne the brunt of Army Group B's attack and they all had their three regiments in the front line with no immediate reserves. Middleton came up with a simple three-point defensive plan for VIII Corps to follow during the early days of the attack:

1 Front line troops had to hold on as long as possible, blocking as many roads as possible.
2 Corps reserves and engineers had to set up roadblocks for stragglers to fall back on.
3 New reinforcements would defend key towns, including St Vith, Houffalize and Bastogne.

VIII Corps only had one armored combat command and four engineer combat battalions in reserve and they set to work preparing roadblocks ahead of the German advance. Time after time a lone tank or anti-tank gun and a few stragglers would bring a kampfgruppe to a halt. At other times engineers blew up a bridge forcing the German armour to take another route or wait until it was repaired. Every delay gave Allied reserves more time to get to the Ardennes.

Although SHAEF promised plenty of reserves, VIII Corps had to manage with what it had for the time being. In the north, 7th Armored Division was heading for St Vith, while 82nd Airborne Division was expected to occupy Houffalize. To the south, 101st Airborne Division and 10th Armored Division were heading for Bastogne.

It was a difficult time for everyone under General Hodges' command. Rumours were rife across First US Army's rear area as stragglers filtered back, telling tales of a massive German breakthrough. The lack of accurate information meant that lurid stories of German spies moving at will, units being overrun and massacres travelled quickly and they grew with every telling. A logistical nightmare also loomed as supply dumps and medical installations had to be moved day after day to stop them falling into German hands.

*Crews from 630th Tank Destroyer Battalion are forced to fight on as foot troops after losing their vehicles. The battalion fought alongside 28th Division in Wiltz on the road to Bastogne. (NARA 111-SC-198296)*

## Sixth Panzer Army Finally Breaks Out

By 18 December I SS Panzer Corps was embarrassed by the failure to reach Elsenborn and 12th SS Panzer Division's armour redoubled its efforts to capture Rocherath and Krinkelt. Time after time they attacked 99th Division's positions but there was little room for manoeuvre. Small groups of German tanks, assault guns and halftracks loaded with panzer grenadiers repeatedly pierced through the American lines but each time they were driven off. The GIs found that their 57-mm battalion anti-tank guns were useless against the German tanks while heavier towed anti-tank guns were easy targets. The infantry usually relied on mines to immobilise a tank, before moving in for the kill with their bazookas.

By the afternoon of the 18th, Dietrich decided it was time to attack the south side of the Elsenborn salient to open the Malmédy road. While 3rd Panzer Grenadier took over the fight for Rocherath and Krinkelt, 12th SS Panzer Division disengaged and moved to Butgenbach. 99th Division and 2nd Division took advantage of the lull in the fighting to evacuate the devastated villages and withdraw back to a new line covering Elsenborn Ridge. The battle had exhausted both sides but the delay to I SS Panzer Corps would have far-reaching repercussions on Sixth Panzer Army's advance.

Throughout 19 December 12th SS Panzer Division and 12th VG Division probed 2nd Division's positions at Butgenbach while

---

Pfc. Richard E. Cowan of 23rd Regiment, 2nd Division, fought on alone while his comrades withdrew to new positions around Krinkelt, driving off 80 infantry and a King Tiger tank. He was killed while covering a second withdrawal. Cowan was awarded the Medal of Honor.

Technician Truman Kimbro's squad was ordered to mine a vital crossroads in Rocherath only to find it occupied by German troops. Kimbro crawled forward under fire to lay the mines, continuing his work after he was seriously wounded; he was killed while crawling to safety. Kimbro was awarded the Medal of Honor.

3rd Parachute Division did the same at Waimes. The main attacks started the following day and although many American positions were overrun, heavy artillery fire helped to drive the Germans back each time. The number of shells fired at the Butgenbach area over an eight-hour period was estimated at 10,000 rounds.

By 21 December 12th SS Panzer Division had virtually run out of armoured vehicles and was unable to make further attacks. Rather than only taking five days to make the 50-mile dash to the Meuse, it had advanced only five miles. LXVII Corps took over the Elsenborn sector the following day when I SS Panzer Corps was ordered south to the Bastogne area. Meanwhile, V Corps had done what had been asked of it by restricting the northern shoulder of the German salient. It had four infantry divisions in a huge arc around Elsenborn and they were backed up by a massive amount of artillery.

Fifteen miles to the west of Elsenborn, 1st SS Panzer Regiment spent the night of 17/18 December outside Stavelot, unaware that there was only a small American garrison in the town. Major Paul J. Solis and his company of armoured infantry entered the town just as Peiper's troops renewed their attack the following morning in a one sided battle, which lasted until the GIs withdrew at midday.

One of Stolis' platoons went north along the Spa road, finding a huge stockpile of gasoline at Francorchamps. They poured 120,000 gallons into a dip in the road and created an enormous flaming roadblock across 1st SS Panzer Regiment's route north. It meant that Peiper had to send twenty tanks west along the Amblève to find an alternative route.

## The German Offensive

As Peiper's tanks negotiated the tortuous road to Trois Ponts, an engineer company was busy building roadblocks to protect the town's three bridges. Major Robert B. Yates had stopped a passing antitank gun team belonging to 7th Armored Division while his men prepared the bridges for demolition. He sent the team to cover the

> One infantry battalion commander at Butenbach later reported: 'The artillery did a great job. I don't know where they got the ammo or when they took time out to flush the guns, but we wouldn't be here now if it wasn't for them ... A hundred [Germans] came at one platoon and not one of them got through.'

*The fear of infiltration continued for days after Skorzeny's men were finally rounded up. Here a checkpoint verifies a driver's papers at Namur on the River Meuse. (NARA 111-SC-198429)*

Stavelot road with their 57-mm gun, with orders to fire warning shots when they saw the Germans approaching.

When Peiper's tanks came into view the anti-tank gun opened fire, immobilising one. The sound of gunfire alerted Yate's engineers, and they demolished the three bridges, one after another. With the way over the Amblève and Salm Rivers barred, all the tanks could do was to turn back to Stavelot and rejoin the rest of the kampfgruppe as it followed a side road towards Werbomont. As Peiper's column passed through La Gleize and crossed the Amblève at Cheneux, the skies cleared leaving the vehicles vulnerable to air attack. It did not take long before they were spotted and US Air Force fighter bombers were soon picking off tanks and halftracks.

Despite the dangers, Peiper's men carried on and by nightfall they were only three miles from Werbomont and the main road north to Liège. 1st SS Panzer Regiment was so near yet so far when American engineers blew the main bridge over the Lienne stream. Peiper's heavy tanks were trapped and while assault guns and half-tracks could cross using a smaller bridge, they were ambushed at Chevron. Another road out of the Amblève valley was closed. All Peiper could do was send his advance guard through the dark along the last road out of the valley, the one towards Stoumont.

The scout planes which had tracked Peiper's column reported the information to First US Army. Radio contact with I SS Panzer

---

Corporal Henry F. Warner had already knocked out two German tanks in front of Butgenbach when his anti-tank gun jammed. He climbed onboard an approaching tank and shot the commander, forcing it to withdraw. Warner was killed on 21 December taking on another tank even though he had been injured; he was awarded the Medal of Honor.

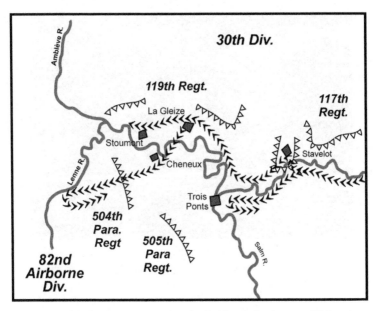

*By the 19th, Peiper was trapped in the Amblève valley between 30th and 82nd Airborne. He believed he had come close to breaking out: 'If we had captured the bridge at Trois Ponts intact and had had enough fuel, it would have been a simple matter to drive though to the Meuse early that day.'*

Corps headquarters had been cut for some time and Sixth Panzer Army had been forced to listen into American radio reports to track Peiper's progress.

While the head of Peiper's column was trapped, there were important developments along his supply lines. Bradley had instructed 30th Division to join V Corps around Eupen but concerns over Peiper's rapid advance resulted in new orders for Major General Leland S. Hobbs. 117th Regiment was directed to form a line of outposts between Stavelot and Malmédy to maintain link between V and VIII Corps.

On the morning of 18 December Lieutenant Colonel Ernest Frankland's battalion headed to Stavelot knowing that Peiper's column had already passed through. His men passed the burning

*One of Peiper's King Tigers covers the bridge at Stavelot. It was finally demolished on the night of 19 December after heavy fighting. (NARA 111-SC-198340)*

roadblock at Francorchamps to find only a token German garrison in the town. Peiper had not thought to hold it because he believed 3rd Parachute Division was following his route. He was wrong and Stavelot was about to be attacked.

The group of tanks forced to turn back from Trois Ponts rolled into Stavelot as Frankland's men cleared the town, but American fighter bombers flying overhead turned the tables, knocking out some German tanks and forcing the rest to seek cover. Frankland's men held on and secured the town the following day. Peiper's ordered the road to be opened on the 19th but American engineers wired the bridge for demolition as his men attacked. I SS Panzer Corps' hopes of reaching the Meuse ended as the Stavelot bridge crashed into the Amblève.

Peiper's supply lines were cut, his vehicles were short of fuel and his men were running out of ammunition. First US Army also knew where his kampfgruppe was while two American divisions were closing in. Although Peiper's men knew they were in a desperate position, they fought on. 30th Division ordered 120th Regiment to dig in between Malmédy to Waimes while 119th Regiment extended the line west along the Amblève valley to Stoumont. As two of 119th Regiment's battalions dug in around Stoumont late on 18 December they were unaware that they blocked Peiper's only escape route.

The kampfgruppe attacked at dawn and while it captured the village, it could not advance any farther west. Peiper did not know that only a single battalion and a handful of tanks stood in his way and Hobbs' men had to rely on artillery fire to stop the German attacks. Eventually Peiper was forced to order his armour back to La Gleize because they were running out of fuel and there would be no more. Liège was still twenty miles away.

## Fifth Panzer Army Closes in on St Vith and Bastogne

St Vith was twelve miles west of 106th Division's front line on Schnee Eifel when Fifth Panzer Army attacked on 16 December. While I SS Panzer Corps was to pass north of the town and LVIII Panzer Corps to the south, LXVI Corps had to capture it. On the evening of 16 December only 168th Engineer Battalion was in the town and the following morning it was ordered to dig in two miles to the east, covering the road to Schönberg. When 14th Cavalry Group fell back through their positions the engineers learnt that a German column was following close behind.

While the engineers dug in and waited, reinforcements were on their way to St Vith. CCB, 9th Armored Division, was already moving through the town, heading south to help 424th Regiment along the River Our around Steinebrück. Meanwhile, 7th Armored Division was making its way along busy roads towards Vielsalm having just missed running into Peiper's kampfgruppe in the Amblève valley.

So far, news of the situation about the disaster on Schnee Eiffel was sketchy but the traffic jams told a sorry tale. Rumours of a German breakthrough were backed up by stories of retreats and surrenders, leaving Major General Robert W. Hasbrouck wondering if his troops could get to St Vith in time. Plans to counterattack towards

Schnee Eiffel were abandoned after the engineer's roadblock was attacked; Hasbrouck's men had to defend St Vith. While 87th Cavalry Reconnaissance Squadron joined the engineers on the afternoon of the 17th, the rest of the division spent the evening forcing their way through the traffic jam to reach the town.

7th Armored Division rolled through St .Vith during the night and while CCB dug in to the east, CCA strung out roadblocks west back towards Vielsalm where CCR was in reserve. 106th Division's 424th Regiment and CCB, 9th Armored Division also pulled back across the River Our, extending the perimeter to the south of the town.

Although St Vith was safe, 106th Division's two regiments on Schnee Eiffel were not. After hearing that a counterattack towards Schönberg was being organised, both regiments destroyed their equipment and headed west to meet it, leaving medics behind with the seriously wounded. News that CCB, 9th Armored Division's counterattack had been cancelled did not reach the two regiments until it was too late. Their attack was a disaster and as casualties mounted and ammunition ran out, it was clear they were not going to get to Schönberg; all they could do was surrender. By dusk around 7,000 men had been taken prisoner; only 150 made it back to St Vith. Neither division nor corps headquarters knew what had happened; only that something had gone terribly wrong.

7th Armored Division had reached the St Vith area in the nick of time. Part of 1st SS Panzer Division was heading for Vielsalm when

A promised Allied air drop never took place on Schnee Eifel. Bad weather grounded half of IX Troop Carrier Command's aircraft in England. While twenty flew into Belgium airspace, they discovered that that no fighter cover had been arranged and they were forced to turn back, leaving the infantry on the ground to fend for themselves.

> Hasbrouck's headquarters remained upbeat about the
> St Vith situation: 'All division units holding firm. Units to
> south have apparently been by-passed by some Boche …
> I have no contact with Corps … but Corps has ordered
> us to hold and situation is well in hand … Hope to see
> you soon … Hope you don't think I'm crazy. C.G. was well
> pleased with everything you have done. Congrats … Don't
> move 'til you hear from me.'

its reconnaissance troops ran into CCR, 7th Armored Division at Recht during the early hours of 18 December. After a fierce fight, the Americans withdrew to Poteau while the rest of SS kampfgruppe deployed and attacked. Both sides suffered heavy casualties and by the time Colonel Duggan gave the order to withdraw, the hamlet was littered with wrecked vehicles and corpses. Mohnke changed his plan when CCA, 7th Armored Division counterattacked in the afternoon and his column turned north towards Stavelot to follow Peiper. 9th SS Panzer Division renewed the attack on 19 December but CCA refused to withdraw and the fierce battle for Poteau ended in a bloody stalemate.

When LXVI Corps started probing Hasbrouck's eastern perimeter, it was clear that 106th Division was not coming back. German troops were closing in on three sides through the thick fog as the battle of St Vith unfolded. While 18th VG Division engaged the roadblock astride the Schönberg road, the attacks north and south of the town never materialised. Führer Begleit Brigade was stuck in traffic to the north while 62nd VG Division needed a bridge over the Our River to the south.

The breakthrough in LVIII Panzer Corps sector to the southeast of St Vith started on 18 December. 116th Panzer Division exploited the breakthrough at Heinerscheid and drove west through Trois Vierges, forcing 112th Regiment to escape north towards St Vith. As 116th Panzer Division forged ahead towards Houffalize, it began to threaten 7th Armored Division's rear.

*Soldiers of the 23rd Armored Infantry Battalion crawl forward along a snow-covered road in their camouflage suits. The battalion formed part of 7th Armored Division's stalwart defence of St Vith. (NARA 111-SC-199032)*

28th Division's thin line was crumbling in front of Fifth Panzer Army's right flank and by nightfall on 17 December XLVII Panzer Corps was driving 110th Regiment back from the River Clerf towards Bastogne. The regimental headquarters held onto Clerf châteaux until the afternoon of the 18th; only then could 2nd Panzer Division head west towards Bastogne.

Panzer Lehr Division suffered similar delays to the south, where it took until midday on 18 December to clear Consthum. Wiltz was next and Colonel Daniel B. Strickler had orders to hold it with a mixed group of engineers, headquarters troops and stragglers supported by a few crippled tanks, for as long as possible. The attacks started on the afternoon of 18 December but 26th VG Division took over the following morning, allowing Panzer Lehr Division to head west. 5th Parachute Division also joined in from the southeast and by nightfall on 19 December the town was all but surrounded. Colonel Strickler ordered the garrison to leave in small groups and head west during the night, confident that he had delayed XLVII Panzer Corps for long enough.

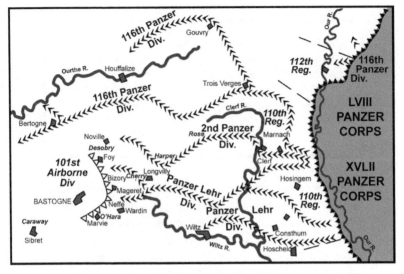

*The advance on Bastogne, 16–19 December. After a disappointing start, Fifth Panzer Army's armour broke through 28th Division's lines and headed west, only to find more roadblocks in front of Bastogne.*

110th Regiment's heroic defences of Clerf and Wiltz had given CCR, 9th Armored Division time to establish roadblocks in the villages east of Bastogne. 2nd Panzer Division now faced three task forces instead an open road through the town. Task Force Rose (Captain L. K. Rose) set up one at Lullange on the Clerf road while Task Force Harper (Lieutenant Colonel Ralph S. Harper) blocked the junction with the Wiltz road at Allerborn. Task Force Booth, (Lieutenant Colonel Robert M. Booth) deployed between Allerborn and Bourcy.

Task Force Rose stopped 2nd Panzer Division's reconnaissance troops the following morning but two tank battalions soon threatened to overrun it. Although Rose's armoured infantry were allowed to withdraw the tanks were ordered to stay until nightfall, when they made a run through the German cordon under cover of darkness. 2nd Panzer Division then took Task Force Harper by surprise (Harper was killed), overrunning it before turning

> Colonel Gilbreth's telephone message to VIII Corps summed
> up Rose's desperate situation; 'Task Force Rose is as good as
> surrounded.... have counted sixteen German tanks there
> ... Task Force is being hit from three sides. Recommend that
> they fight their way out ... Plan to push Task Force Rose
> toward the other road block. If the decision is to stay, some
> units will be sent there to help them out.'

northwest towards Bourcy, cutting off Task Force Booth. Booth's
men were forced to make a run for it into nearby woods but
only a few men made it back to Bastogne. Although CCR's three
roadblocks had been overrun, they had held up XLVIII Panzer
Corps for a day; another day for VIII Corps to deploy its reserves.

The delays allowed time for Team Desobry (Major William
R. Desobry) from 10th Armored Division to occupy Noville.
Desobry's men repeatedly drove back 2nd Panzer Division's attacks
throughout 19 December, including one by over 30 tanks, and
continued to hold on through the night. Despite Manteuffel's high
hopes for 2nd Panzer Division, it had advanced only ten miles in
two days.

Although VIII Corps headquarters had moved from Bastogne to
Neufchâteau, Middleton remained behind to supervise the defence
of the town. While Panzer Lehr Division was fighting to capture
Wiltz, CCR, 9th Division had set up roadblocks at Longvilly and
Mageret, Neffe and Marvie. Team Cherry (Lieutenant Colonel Henry
T. Cherry) of CCB, 10th Armored Division, was also sent forward to
reinforce Longvilly and Neffe on the afternoon of the 19th. They had
to hold on long enough to allow reserves to reach Bastogne.

Panzer Lehr Division finally headed out of the Wiltz valley during
the afternoon on 19 December. Bayerlein had to personally untangle
the traffic jam as his vehicles squeezed past 26th VG Division on the
road to Bastogne. He correctly assessed that the main road through

*Some men discovered that the new snowsuits could be too effective and these GIs have painted large circles on their backs to aid identification and prevent accidents. (NARA 111-SC-199634)*

Longvilly would be guarded and directed his leading kampfgruppe along a side road, bypassing Longvilly and heading towards Mageret. At the same time part of Team Cherry was moving into Longvilly while the rest of it stayed behind in Neffe, only two miles from Bastogne's centre. The battle for Bastogne's eastern perimeter had started and while 101st Airborne Division was close by, it needed another day to establish a perimeter around the town.

So could Team Cherry delay Panzer Lehr Division long enough to give the paratroopers the time they needed?

## Countering Seventh Army's Attack along the Sauer

By 18 December LXXXV Corps, on Seventh Army's right, was struggling to keep up with Fifth Panzer Army's advance. While 5th Parachute Division had advanced twelve miles and joined the battle at Wiltz, 352nd VG Division was ten miles behind around Führen. Meanwhile, VIII Corps was having its own problems and as 109th Regiment withdrew through Diekirch to Ettelbrück, it moved away from the rest of 28th Division, creating a large gap in VIII Corps' line.

CCA, 9th Armored Division had just arrived in the area and General Leonard ordered it to counterattack 276th VG Division immediately. Task Force Hall and Task Force Philbeck advanced before dawn on the 18th but they ran straight into German battle groups waiting for their own attack to begin. Although Leonard had to call his counterattack off, jeeps continued to find ways through the German lines to reach the isolated front line companies and they spent all day taking ammunition forward, returning with wounded men.

To the south, CCA, 9th Armored Division was ordered to withdraw to a new defensive line through Waldbillig, Ermsdorf and Ettelbrück on the night of 18/19 December. Although the move

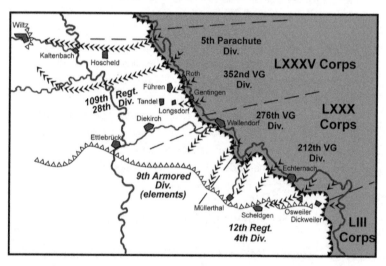

*Seventh Army's battle, 16–19 December. While LXXXV Corps broke through 28th Division on Seventh Army's right, LXXX Corps struggled to establish a bridgehead across the River Sauer.*

*Private Peter Stulgis of 51st Combat Engineer Battalion carries out the final checks on to explosive charges before withdrawing from the Echternach area. When detonated they would bring down the trees across the road, delaying the German advance. (NARA 111-SC-198397)*

extended the gap in VIII Corps' line, 276th VG Division was not in a position to exploit it because its assault guns had not crossed the Sauer. Although the infantry captured Waldbillig they could not advance farther.

The arrival of CCA, 10th Armored Division in 4th Division's area on the night of 17/18th December, was significant because they were the first reinforcements from Third US Army. Early on 18 December CCA sent three task forces forward through 12th Regiment's lines, hoping to recover the lost ground on 4th Division's left flank. Task Force Chamberlain had a daunting task as it edged down the narrow Schwarz Erntz ravine in single file while Task Force Luckett cleared the bluffs either side of the gorge. Task Force Standish ran into stiff German resistance in Berdorf but Task Force Riley reached the edge of Echternach, finding 12th Regiment's infantry still holding part of the town. 212th VG Division was also still waiting for its armour to cross the river and its infantry were unable to exploit the gap around Scheidgen. Now that 10th Armored Division was closing in, the initiative would soon be handed over to the Americans.

# 20–21 December
# The Battles for St Vith and Bastogne

## SHAEF Makes Command Changes

As the situation along First US Army's front deteriorated, there were alterations afoot for SHAEF's command of the Ardennes battlefield. While V Corps was holding its own, Army Group B was forcing a huge wedge in VIII Corps' sector, making it difficult for General Bradley to control both sides of the salient. On 20 December Eisenhower decided to divide control of the battlefield between two Army Groups to make it easier to command.

The decision was discussed in detail the following morning and the dividing line was drawn from Givet on the River Meuse forward to St Vith at the front line. Field Marshal Montgomery's 21st Army Group would take over control of First and Ninth US Armies and hold the northern shoulder of the developing 'Bulge'. Bradley's 12th Army Group would counterattack from the southern shoulder as soon as Third US Army was ready.

Dividing the battlefield in two was a sensible strategic move because command and control of such a large area was becoming impossible for one army group headquarters. Lines of communications were stretched to breaking point and the split would allow each Army Group commander to concentrate on his own part of the battlefield. Involving 21st Army Group in the battle would also encourage Montgomery to deploy British reserves to the Ardennes.

It was a difficult decision for Eisenhower to make and while neither Lieutenant General Walter Bedell Smith, Eisenhower's Chief of Staff, nor General Bradley liked the idea, they both concurred.

> There was a similar division of the Allied air forces as for the ground forces. While IX and XXIX US Tactical Air Commands reported to the British Second Tactical Air Force in the north, part of IX Tactical Air Command was added to XIX Tactical Air Command in the south.

But while the generals put their differences aside the politicians and press reacted strongly, questioning why two US Armies had been placed under British command.

Montgomery immediately visited Hodges with news that XXX British Corps was moving its five divisions south to guard the Meuse bridges. He made it clear that V Corps had to hold onto Elsenborn to anchor the northern shoulder and CCA, 3rd Armored Division, was moving up to give it support. CCB, 3rd Armored Division, was also moving to reinforce XVIII Airborne Corps' line along the Amblève and Salm rivers. Lieutenent General Matthew B. Ridgway's corps was also given responsibility for the St Vith salient. It had to establish a new defensive line between Vielsalm and Hotton, ready for when the salient had to be evacuated. This reallocation of corps sectors increased XVIII Airborne Corps sector from 25 to a massive 85 miles. Lieutenant General J. Lawton Collins' VII Corps was also moving to join First US Army with orders to extend its line west from Hotton to Rochefort, right in front of Fifth Panzer Army's advance.

In 12th Army Group's sector, Third US Army was preparing to counterattack Army Group B's southern flank. Patton had been moving troops towards the Ardennes for several days and he planned to relieve Bastogne, cutting across Fifth Panzer and Seventh Army's lines of communications. Although plenty of American and British troops were heading to the Ardennes by 20 December, the question was would they plug the huge gap between XVIII Airborne Corps and VIII Corps before Fifth Panzer Army reached the Meuse?

When VIII Corps was transferred to Third US Army's command, 9th Armored Division's CCB was given orders to leave Bastogne and head west to St Hubert. General Middleton was in the town when the order came through and he disagreed with Patton, cancelling the move; his decision would change the course of the battle in the Allies' favour.

## Containing Sixth Army's Breakout

By 21 December it was stalemate around Stoumont and while 1st SS Panzer Regiment could not move due to a lack of fuel, Hobbs' troops could make any headway. Although part of CCB, 3rd Armored Division, joined the fight neither Task Force McGeorge nor Task Force Jordan could break through the kampfgruppe's perimeter. However, Task Force Lovelady cut the road to Stavelot, and dug in across 1st SS Panzer Regiment's escape route. Although Peiper's dwindling group of men was surrounded, they were still dangerous, as 504th Parachute Regiment discovered when attacked Cheneux.

After waiting in traffic jams behind the lines for several days, it was clear that Skorzeny was never going to have the opportunity to capture the Meuse bridges. Instead, Dietrich ordered 150th Panzer Brigade to capture Malmédy and open the road to Liège. During the morning fog of 21 December, a mixture of vehicles, some American and some German models modified to look American, moved towards 120th Regiment's perimeter accompanied by infantry dressed in a mixture of US and German uniforms. However, a deserter had compromised the attack and 120th Regiment was waiting. Both of 150th Panzer Brigade assault groups were stopped in their tracks.

XVIII Airborne Corps still had to secure a defensive line from Vielsalm on the Amblève River, southwest through Manhay to La Roche on the Ourthe River. It was a huge gap and while

*A chaplain holds an impromptu service for a group from 504th Parachute Regiment as the 82nd Airborne Division moves towards Cheneux. (NARA 111-SC-200715)*

During the attack on Malmédy, Sergeant Francis Currey used a bazooka to knock out one tank before using anti-tank grenades to force three tank crews to abandon their vehicles. After climbing onto a half-track and using the machine gun, he used another abandoned machine gun to drive German infantry back, allowing five trapped comrades to escape. Nineteen-year-old Currey was awarded the Medal of Honor.

82nd Airborne Division and part of 3rd Armored Division were heading towards the area, so was LVIII Panzer Corps. No one knew where Krüger's corps was but General Ridgway was about to find out.

Major General James M. Gavin had orders to cover the 25-mile gap between Hotton and Stoumont with his 82nd Airborne Division but there were many roads for his airborne soldiers to guard. While 504th Parachute Regiment headed towards La Gleize to join the battle against Peiper, 505th Parachute Regiment moved towards Trois Ponts to cover the Salm River. 508th Parachute Regiment moved to Vielsalm to make contact with 7th Armored Division's perimeter around St Vith. To the west, 325th Glider Regiment moved to Manhay and Fraiture, sending one battalion to guard Hotton with CCR, 3rd Armored Division.

As Gavin's men moved northeast, Ridgway was pleased to hear they had not encountered any Germans between Manhay and Vielsalm. While that was good news, the bad news was that 116th Panzer Division was at Houffalize and heading northwest towards Hotton.

## Fifth Panzer Army Attacks St Vith

Wooded ridges dictated the organisation of Hasbrouck's perimeter around St Vith. CCA, 7th Armored Division, was to the north and northwest, CCB, 7th Armored Division, was to the east while CCB, 9th Armored Division and 424th Regiment were to the south. Hasbrouck found it difficult to keep in touch with them all and radio communications with VIII Corps and XVIII Airborne Corps were also patchy. The only consolation was his men had spent the last two days digging in.

The American artillery batteries used the new POZIT proximity fuse for the first time during the attack on Malmédy. The shell casings contained a radio device which allowed the explosive to detonate just a few metres above ground, something gunners had previously had to estimate using timed fuses. The high frequency of ground bursts decimated Skorzeny's troops.

The delays around St Vith were becoming embarrassing for Fifth Panzer Army because while LVIII Panzer Corps was making good progress through Houffalize, LXVI Corps was over 20 miles behind. The attack on St Vith finally started on 20 December but traffic congestion again interfered with Lucht's plans. Führer Begleit Brigade's tanks could not get through and its infantry failed to make any gains around Hunningen north of the town. 62nd VG Division's attack to the southeast did not get anywhere either. In the centre 18th VG Division also waited all day and postponed its attack when it was clear that its artillery batteries could not get into position. By the end of the day the American perimeter was still holding and Manteuffel was losing his patience with Lucht.

Meanwhile 82nd Airborne Division had reached Vielsalm, making contact with 7th Armored Division's perimeter. However, Hasbrouck still had plenty to worry about on his open south flank,

*A patrol creeps through the woods looking for German outposts; the GIs' new snow capes help them blend into the snowy landscape. (NARA 111-SC-198162)*

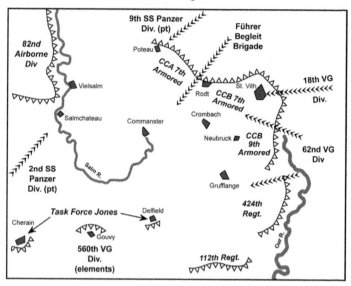

*LXVI Corps struggled to break through 7th Armored Division's perimeter around St Vith, 18–21 December.*

especially when he heard that 2nd SS Panzer Division had turned north from Houffalize and was heading for Salmchâteau to cut off his escape routes.

Hasbrouck only had Task Force Jones to spare to stop 2nd SS Panzer Division and it split into three tiny detachments to cover the six mile gap south of Bouvigny. While they were not expected to stop 2nd SS Panzer Division, Hasbrouck hoped they might be able to delay it and raise the alarm. The first detachment found Deifeld unoccupied and the second scattered a small German garrison in Cherain but the third found Gouvy in enemy hands and opted to block the roads either side.

LXVI Corps renewed its pincer attack against St Vith on the afternoon of 21 December but Führer Begleit Brigade's armour was still stuck in traffic jams, leaving the infantry to fight through the the American lines near Rodt for a second time. Although 62nd VG Division now joined the attack, it failed to capture Maldingen.

> Task Force Jones found Lieutenant Colonel Stone's
> service troops and a group of stragglers at Gouvy
> railhead depot. Hasbrouck sent lorries to move the
> stores to St Vith, allowing him to lift rationing on food,
> water and gasoline. Stone also handed over 350 German
> prisoners he had taken.

While the two pincer attacks against St Vith failed, 18th VG Division broke though astride the Schönberg road, in the centre of Hasbrouck's perimeter. The division's tanks cut Colonel William H. G. Fuller's position in two, overrunning four armoured infantry companies in no time; over 600 men were killed or captured and less than 200 men escaped.

As Fuller's men fell back, two tank destroyers stood in the way of 18th VG Division's advance, stopping any German tanks entering St Vith until midnight. The heroic last stand gave CCB, 7th Armored Division, time to withdraw to a new defensive line south west of the town prepared by Lieutenant Colonels Robert C. Erlenbusch and Robert L. Rhea. Although the first stage of the evacuation from the St Vith pocket had been successful, 7th Armored Division had a long way to go before it was safe.

## Fifth Panzer Army Breaks Out West of Houffalize

VIII Corps' plan to hold Houffalize with 82nd Airborne Division had been abandoned due to the speed of Fifth Panzer Army's advance. Instead, Middleton sent engineers to block the roads around Hotton, Manhay and Vielsalm and they worked around the clock, preparing bridges for demolition, mining fords, blowing craters and felling trees. Although they built many roadblocks, all too often there were too few troops to defend them.

LVIII Panzer Corps planned to cross the Ourthe west of Houffalize and then head for Marche-en-Famenne, and XVIII Airborne

Corps had to stop it. On 20 December 116th Panzer Division was approaching Houffalize along both banks of the Ourthe. The southern kampfgruppe was in the lead and it turned north at Bertogne, only to find the bridge over the Ourthe in ruins. While engineers spent the afternoon repairing the crossing, troops from 7th Armored Division dug in on the opposite bank. News that the division's reconnaissance troops had found another bridge five miles to west changed the situation but while Waldenburg wanted to use the Ortheuville crossing, Krüger was convinced it was a trap and had other ideas.

116th Panzer Division's northern kampfgruppe had entered Houffalize, finding the town unguarded and the bridge intact. Krüger ordered Waldenburg to switch his southern kampfgruppe to the north bank, using the Houffalize bridge. While the order might have looked simple on a map, it took all night to carry out and 116th Panzer Division lost precious time and wasted precious fuel.

116th Panzer Division's reconnaissance troops then began exploring west of Houffalize and when they ran into one of 7th Armored Division's rearguards in La Roche the news rocked First US Army's headquarters. It meant that LVIII Panzer Corps had access to the road network between the Ourthe and the Salm, threatening the rear of the St Vith salient.

XVIII Airborne Corps had to secure a defensive line between Hotton and Manhay before 116th Panzer Division reached the

Corporal Horace M. Thorne was leading led one of 89th Cavalry Reconnaissance Squadron's patrols towards Grufflange when a German tank was immobilised. He climbed onto it and threw two grenades into the turret, killing the crew before using a machine gun to knock out two machine gun teams, forcing the advancing German infantry to withdraw. Thorne was killed trying to clear his jammed gun; he was awarded the Medal of Honor.

# The German Offensive

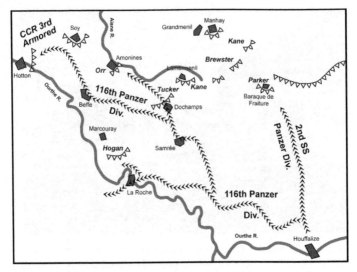

*XLVII Panzer Corps breakout west of Houffalize on 20–21 December threatened First US Army's lines around Hotton and Manhay.*

*Everyone is on guard at one of 3rd Armored Division's roadblocks on the roads around Hotton. Sergeant Tony Stozer keeps a lookout for enemy activity over the top of his .03 calibre machine-gun while Private Milton Forrester watches from the turret of his concealed tank. (NARA 111-SC-199417)*

area but all that Ridgway could spare was CCR, 3rd Armored Division. Major General Maurice Rose split the command into four small columns (Task Forces Hogan, Tucker, Kane and Orr) each based around a reinforced tank company. As the four task forces explored the area between Hotton and Manhay, 116th Panzer Division and 560th VG Division were heading straight towards them.

*Tank crews from 3rd Armored Division inspect two of 116th Panzer Division's tanks knocked out in Hotton having stopped LVIII Corps crossing the Ourthe. A Panzer IV is partially hidden behind the Panther tank. (NARA 111-SC-197822)*

Hogan drove along the east bank of the Ourthe River and while 7th Armored Division troops were holding La Roche, one of 116th Panzer Division's roadblocks was to the south. Kane did not encounter any German troops southeast of Manhay, but it had found a small group of stragglers holding Baraque de Fraiture crossroads.

General Rose's main problem was in the centre of his front at Dochamps. Tucker ran into a group of supply troops who had abandoned their supply dump in Samrée when German tanks appeared. Shortly afterwards Tucker's men were also engaged in a desperate battle to stop them reaching Amonines and all Rose could do was send Task Force Orr forward to help. The battle lasted until nightfall when Waldenburg withdrew his armour and allowed them to use the 25,000 gallons of gasoline stored at Samrée depot.

By now General Rose knew the direction of 116th Panzer Division advance but he had no more troops to stop it; his combat command would have to fight on alone.

## Fifth Panzer Army Bypasses Bastogne

2nd Panzer Division spent a second day trying to take Noville to the north of Bastogne, only to see Team Harwick (Major Robert F. Harwick had taken over when Desobry was wounded) escape into the town at dusk. The tiny group of GIs had held an armoured division at bay for two days. Night had fallen on 20 December when General Lauchert reported that 2nd Panzer Division was ready to start moving. Although he asked for permission to turn south to attack the 101st Airborne Division's perimeter, General Lüttwitz told him to 'forget Bastogne and head for the Meuse!'

2nd Panzer Division's reconnaissance battalion headed west towards Ortheuville to cross the undamaged bridge discovered by 116th Panzer Division. As the first German vehicle crossed the river, American engineers on the far bank pushed the detonator; but nothing happened, the demolition charges had failed. The vehicle then came under a hail of fire, stopping it in its tracks in the middle of the bridge. A desperate battle followed but the rest of the battalion forced a way across allowing the rest of 2nd Panzer Division to cross the river during the night.

Waldenburg was able to report that his armour was assembled near Tenneville, only ten miles from Marche-en-Famenne and in striking distance of the road north to Namur. 2nd Panzer Division only had to cross another 30 miles of open country before it reached Namur at the confluence of the River Sambre and River Meuse; and there were no American troops in front of it.

84th Division had been allocated to VII Corps but it had just reached Marche and by dawn on 21 December only one regiment was digging in around the town. Collins expected 2nd Panzer Division to attack but as the hours passed nothing happened; Lauchert's armour spent all day waiting for fuel supplies. It gave time for the rest of 84th Division and part of CCA, 3rd Armored Division to form a defensive line between Hotton, Marche and Rochefort.

*General 'Lightning Joe' Lawton Collins, VII Corps commander, observes the German positions from a forward observation post; he is accompanied by his nephew, a member of VII Corps staff. (NARA 111-SC-198682)*

While 2nd Panzer Division had made good progress, the rest of Lüttwitz's corps still had to capture Bastogne. 26th VG Division was surprised to find Team Cherry holding Longvilly early on 20 December and it took time to coordinate an attack with Panzer Lehr Division. Cherry's men evacuated the village late in the afternoon only to find Panzer Lehr's column blocking their escape route through Mageret and Neffe, forcing them they had to abandon their vehicles and escape on foot. Panzer Lehr Division attacked the rest of Task Force Cherry in Neffe at the same time but yet again Cherry's men fought on until late afternoon. Cherry finally had to report; 'We are pulling out … We're not driven out but burned out.'

## 101st Airborne Division Moves into Bastogne

While Team Cherry fought Lüttwitz's corps to a standstill to the east of Bastogne, others were approaching the town from the west. 82nd and 101st Airborne Divisions division had been refitting near

Reims when the German attack began and departed in a rush. The paratroopers had no time to prepare and they only carried what ammunition they had to hand. They also left a lot of equipment behind, hoping that there would be supplies waiting for them at their destinations.

As the two divisions headed towards VIII Corps front, Middleton was waiting in Bastogne. He correctly believed that Fifth Panzer Army needed the town's road network if it was to maintain its advance and he planned to hold it for as long as possible. 9th Armored Division's CCR was already east of the town and 101st Division was expected to form a defensive perimeter.

Middleton was going to direct 82nd Airborne Division to Houffalize, eleven miles north of Bastogne, but the threat from 1st SS Panzer Division moving along the Amblève valley took precedence. General Gavin's paratroopers headed for Werbomont to stop Kampfgruppe Peiper reaching the Meuse. Meanwhile, 101st Airborne Division assembled west of Bastogne around midnight on 19th after a difficult journey.

Middleton immediately ordered General Anthony C. McAuliffe, 101st Division's artillery commander, (Major-General Maxwell D. Taylor was on leave in the United States) to start forming a perimeter around the town at first light on 20 December. As 501st Parachute Regiment moved through the town Colonel Julian

Airborne divisions were smaller than infantry divisions and had less support weapons. Although they had three parachute regiments and one glider regiment they only had three light pack howitzer battalions and one 105-mm howitzer battalion. They did not have large amounts of organic transportation either and the paratroopers were driven through the night to Bastogne on a variety of commandeered trucks.

J. Ewell was aware there had been heavy fighting to the east but he did not know the full tactical situation. As Cherry's men fell back from Longvilly and Neffe they met Ewell's paratroopers moving out of Bastogne, and their covering fire stopped Panzer Lehr's infantry in their tracks. The timely arrival of the paratroopers meant that Fifth Panzer Army could not walk straight into Bastogne, but there was still a long way to go before the town was safe.

McAuliffe's men spent 20 December making their way through the town, pushing through the jam of vehicles and men, to reach their allotted positions on the perimeter. As the paratroopers dug into the frozen ground, XLVII Panzer Corps was moving to the north and south and by the morning of 21 December 101st Airborne Division was trapped inside a rough circle, around five miles in diameter. 502nd Parachute Regiment was to the north and 506th Parachute Regiment to the northeast. 501st Parachute Regiment was east of the town and 327th Glider Regiment and the divisional engineers were to the south and west.

McAuliffe placed the division's organic artillery, two battalions of 155-mm and a mobile armored field artillery battalion southwest of the town with the division trains and service companies. There were a mixture of armoured units in the town, including Colonel William L. Roberts' 10th Armored Division's CCB and 9th Armored Division's CCR. There was also a tank destroyer battalion and a handful of light tanks and antiaircraft automatic weapons carriers.

Disaster struck during the night of 19 December when a German raid overran 101st Airborne Division's service area at Mande-St Etienne, capturing a large amount of stores and cutting off most of the divisional transport. It left the division short of many important items but many military dumps and civilian stores were found in Bastogne, making up part of the deficit.

Each combat team was formed by a group of paratroopers supported by a mixture of armour and antiaircraft weapons who had found themselves trapped inside the town. Teams were named after their commanding officer but several hundred stragglers were organised as a reserve in the centre of the town and named Team SNAFU (from the soldiers' acronym, Situation Normal, All 'Fouled' Up).

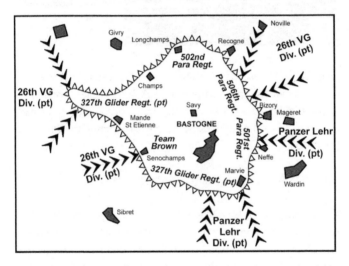

*XLVII Panzer Corps repeatedly attacked 101st Airborne Division's perimeter around Bastogne after 21 December.*

Although McAuliffe's paratroopers rarely fought alongside armour, they soon learned to work with the tank crews.

While 2nd Panzer Division gave 101st Airborne Division's perimeter north of the town a wide berth, Panzer Lehr Division did the same to the south side. It left 26th VG Division to attack alone and while it made a temporary breakthrough between Foy and Bizory in the morning, it took all afternoon to take over the area vacated by Panzer Lehr Division. General Bayerlein left

*These two men belonged to 110th Regiment of the 28th Division that had been overrun by the German advance. The men escaped to Bastogne and joined Team SNAFU. Their faces sum up the situation 'Situation Normal, All Fouled Up'. (NARA 111-SC-198304)*

Kampfgruppe Kunkel behind to help 26th VG Division and the alarm was raised when it overran one of McAuliife's artillery battalions, forcing two howitzer battalions to abandon Villeroux. Team Pyle had to deploy to stop it taking Senonchamps. The battle for Bastogne had begun.

## Third US Army Prepares to Counterattack

When Army Group B's offensive began on 16 December, Third US Army had been planning to attack the West Wall in the Saar area. The offensive was cancelled when Bradley told Patton about the Ardennes situation and 10th Armored Division headed north the following day. Bradley called Patton to his Luxembourg headquarters on 18 December and after hearing about the width and depth of the German penetration, Third US Army's commander offered the 4th Armored, 5th and 80th Infantry Divisions.

Patton met Eisenhower at Verdun the following morning and learnt that First US Army would initially be on the defensive in the north while Third US Army counterattacked from the south. VIII Corps' engineers were currently building roadblocks between Libramont and Martelange, southwest of Bastogne, to allow Third US Army to assemble on Seventh Army's flank.

# The German Offensive

*Private Edward Nobles watches over the top of his frost-covered .03 calibre machine-gun and waits for the next German attack to begin. (NARA 111-SC-199262)*

Patton in turn explained Third US Army's progress and his plans for a counterattack. Four divisions were already moving north, despite the atrocious weather. By midnight on 20 December III Corps would take over the Arlon sector south of Bastogne while XII Corps covered Luxembourg City. Patton wanted his units to attack as soon as they reached the battlefield but Eisenhower ordered him to be patient and to prepare a co-ordinated attack across a wide front.

III Corps would lead the advance towards Bastogne, starting on 22 December, and General John Millikin faced a difficult task. While he knew little of Seventh Army's situation, it was clear that his troops would be advancing through a patchwork of thick woods cut by ravines and watercourses. The weather also changed daily, ranging from snow, ice and clear skies to rain, mud and fog.

Millikin arrived at his Arlon headquarters on 20 December to find 4th Armored Division waiting, having completed a difficult 160-mile drive through huge traffic jams. General Gaffey's tanks and halftracks were worn out and his units were below strength. 26th Infantry Division was also in position but it, too, was not at its best having just received hundreds of replacements; 80th Infantry Division was still moving up from Luxembourg City.

4th Armored Division's CCB was attached to VIII Corps on 20 December and Middleton immediately ordered a task force, composed of a tank company, an armoured infantry company and a battery of self-propelled artillery to drive north towards Bastogne to judge the German reaction. Captain Bert Ezell's small group headed up the Neufchateau road and, to everyone's surprise, it travelled over twenty miles without seeing any Germans. Ezell drove into Bastogne and reported to 101st Airborne Division's headquarters. Although Colonel Roberts wanted Ezell to stay, VIII Corps ordered him to return and he did so, again without seeing the enemy. After seven hours on the road, Ezell's tanks reached their bivouac towing three abandoned artillery pieces behind them. While Ezell was fortunate not to run into the enemy, his uninterrupted journey revealed the fragmented nature of Seventh Army's lines south of Bastogne and begs the question why General Gaffey did not send the rest of CCB into the town; the answer is lost in the fog of war.

## Seventh Army's Battle along the Sauer

By 20 December Seventh Army's advance was divided into two distinct parts: success in LXXXV Corps' area and failure in LXXX Corps' area. 5th Parachute Division resumed its advance once Wiltz fell, moving south of Bastogne. 352nd Division also followed up 109th Regiment's withdrawal from Diekirch and advanced towards Ettelbrück. LXXXV Corps had to stretch its troops to keep in touch with Fifth Panzer Army and while a large gap had opened up in VIII Corps line, General Kniess did not have enough troops to exploit it.

In LXXX Corps' sector 212th VG Division was still trying to consolidate its bridgehead over the Sauer in the face of attacks by CCA, 10th Armored Division. While General Sensfuss' men failed to take Berdorf from Task Force Standish, it forced Task Force Riley to abandon its attempt to reach Echternach. The company of men cut off in the town finally surrendered to 212th VG Division after four days behind enemy lines.

# THE ALLIED COUNTEROFFENSIVE

## Protecting the Meuse Bridges

While reinforcements were moving towards the Ardennes area from all directions, SHAEF continued to summon divisions from far and wide. On 18 December 11th Armored Division was ordered to leave England and head towards the battlefield, with orders to protect the Meuse bridges. Field Marshal Montgomery started moving troops south from 21st Army Group's area the following day; they included XXX Corps, the Guards Armoured Division, 43rd, 51st, 53rd Infantry Divisions and three armoured brigades. On 20 December 6th British Airborne Division was also ordered to

Despite all the precautions and scares only one real threat to the Meuse bridges materialised. On the night of 23 December a small group of Germans dressed in American uniforms drove their jeep as far as Dinant. They were stopped by one of the many checkpoints and were taken prisoner when they failed to give the correct answers. It was a case of too little, too late.

the Continent with orders to deploy along the Meuse. Eisenhower's main concern was that Army Group B might be across the Meuse before the reinforcements reached the river.

There were also worries that German troops dressed as American soldiers or Belgian civilians would take a bridge by stealth. It was possible that there could be another parachute drop along the river while rumours of spies behind the American lines were rife. No one was trusted and security increased to hysterical proportions. Unit passwords were no longer sufficient and checkpoints asked random questions on American sport, history and geography just to make sure.

The first British troops reached the river on 21 December and XXX Corps was soon ready to counterattack if German armour crossed the river. Although Sixth Panzer Army's left flank was stalled along the River Amblève, Dietrich's right wing or Fifth Panzer Army's sector could still reach the Meuse between Namur and Dinant. Engineer units had been mobilized to prepare the bridges for demolition and Brigadier General Charles O. Thrasher had authority to demolish any if German troops approached. By 23 December a thin screen of engineers, artillery and antitank units were dug in along the river while French troops from the Metz garrison manned the string of checkpoints. When 11th Armored Division eventually arrived at the Meuse on 24 December the bridges were finally secure.

While SHAEF assumed that Army Group B intended to cross the River Meuse, there was always a small element of doubt. Fifth Panzer

---

The US Air Force made many bombing raids against Peiper's perimeter but several missed their target by a considerable distance. Malmédy, seven miles to the east, was bombed by accident on the 23rd, 24th and 25th, resulting in many civilian casualties; a general evacuation of the town followed.

Army's could just as easily turn south through Sedan heading for Paris as it could turn north towards Liège and Antwerp. Eisenhower wanted to be sure and on 18 December he ordered 17th Airborne to cross to France and move to the Reims area to protect the Semois and Chiers Rivers. It was delayed by bad weather and it did not reach Charleville until 27 December.

# 22–23 December
# Army Group B's High Water Mark

## The End of Sixth Army's Breakout

By 22 December Kampfgruppe Peiper was cut off in the La Gleize area and running short of fuel and ammunition. Dietrich was anxious to continue pushing forward but 1st SS Panzer Division had to find another way forward since the demolition of the Stavelot bridge. One kampfgruppe tried to cross the Amblève west of Stavelot but the temporary bridge collapsed under the weight of an assault gun while Task Force Lovelady stopped the panzer grenadiers advancing along the riverbank. A second kampfgruppe crossed the River Salm at two places south of Trois Ponts only to run into 505th Parachute Regiment; the panzer grenadiers were forced to evacuate both bridgeheads. CCA, 7th Armored Division, was also still at Poteau, blocking the road to Vielsalm. Further attempts to cross the Salm on the 23rd also had to be abandoned. 1st SS Panzer Regiment was going to have to fight it out on its own.

30th Division resumed the attack on Peiper's perimeter in blizzard conditions on 22 December. Once Task Force Harrison took Stoumont sanatorium it found that Peiper's men had withdrawn from the village back to La Gleize, leaving their wounded behind. By 23 December Peiper's time was up and he gave the order to withdraw. Under cover of darkness 800 able-bodied men left La Gleize, leaving 300 more wounded behind, and waded across the Amblève, hiding in woods north of Trois Ponts during daylight hours. The following night they slipped though

*The cold weather and snow have frozen the ground on Elsenborn Ridge but these GIs of 2nd Infantry Division still need foxholes. Explosive charges are used to break up the soil and give them a head start in their digging. (NARA 111-SC-198592)*

505th Parachute Regiment's lines and crossed the Salm south of Trois Ponts, rejoining 1st SS Panzer Division, south of Stavelot, on Christmas morning.

119th Regiment entered a quiet La Gleize on 24 December, finding Peiper's wounded and 170 American prisoners. The village was strewn with 1st SS Panzer Regiment's wrecked vehicles; 28 tanks, 70 half-tracks, and 25 artillery pieces. It took until 26 December to check that the area was clear.

> SS troops considered themselves superior to regular units and particularly over Volks Grenadier units. They always insisted on having the right of way on the roads, often stopping other artillery and supply units so their own could get through. This SS domination of the road network hampered Lucht's advance west of St Vith, easing 7th Armored Division's withdrawal from the salient.

## Evacuating the St Vith Salient

As Hasbrouck planned his withdrawal from the St Vith salient on 22 December, XVIII Airborne Corps headquarters reported that 2nd SS Panzer Division was moving north from Houffalize towards Task Force Jones' roadblocks. Hasbrouck immediately instructed 424th and 112th Regiments to form roadblocks along the Salm River back to Salmchâteau while the rest of his troops prepared to evacuate the salient. Difficult, because they first had to disengage before withdrawing along a few narrow roads through a forest. Fortunately for Hasbrouck, a scramble for billets and loot after 18th VG Division entered St Vith ruined Lucht's hopes of an easy victory.

There was still a long way to go before 7th Armored Division escaped from the St Vith salient. On the north side CCA, 7th Armored Division, was still holding onto Poteau, stopping 9th SS Panzer Division reaching Vielsalm. Führer Begleit Brigade's armour had finally arrived and managed to cut the road between Poteau and Rodt in blizzard conditions, threatening 7th Armored Division's new defensive position. For a second time Hasbrouck's troops had to fall back to a new line.

Field Marshal Montgomery had just taken over command of First US Army and he found Hasbrouck's summary of the St Vith salient situation very worrying. Roads were poor, men were tired, units were mixed up and the Germans were closing in on three sides. To make matters worse, the escape routes through Vielsalm and Salmchâteau were in danger of being cut. Although

Hasbrouck offered to stand and fight, he favoured an immediate withdrawal; 'In my opinion if we don't get out of here and up north of the 82nd [Airborne Division] before night, we will not have a 7th Armored Division left.'

Montgomery agreed and told Hodges 'They can come back with all honour. They must come back to the more secure positions. They have put up a wonderful show.' On the afternoon of 22 December withdrawal orders were issued, demolitions were laid and rearguards were organised. One last supply column delivered extra fuel, allowing many more vehicles to join the withdrawal, but it was going to be a race against time.

On the north side of the perimeter, CCA, 7th Armored Division, held onto Poteau while CCR, 7th Armored Division, escaped west to Vielsalm. CCA, 7th Armored Division, followed across the Salm while US Air Force planes stopped the Germans armour following.

In the centre, CCB, 9th Armored Division, moved before dawn to Salmchâteau, with Task Force Lindsey acting as its rearguard. Part of CCB, 7th Armored Division, withdrew to Commanster at first light and then followed a frozen forest trail to get to Vielsalm. Task Force Boylan was acting as the rearguard but Führer Begleit Brigade dare not enter the forest and instead used the main road to reach Salmchâteau. The rest of CCB, 7th Armored Division, took advantage of the hard frost to drive cross country and bypass the Germans holding Crombach. They then drove through 62nd VG Division's lines with guns blazing to get to safety. 424th Regiment then broke contact and completed the evacuation of the south side of the St Vith perimeter.

112th Infantry had been holding the area southeast of Salmchâteau but Führer Begleit Brigade forced it out of Rogery back towards Salmchâteau. Colonel Gustin Nelson was watching his men cross the Salm when he saw German tanks approaching his command post; he immediately blew the bridge. Although the demolished bridge left Task Force Jones isolated, he refused to surrender and 200 men fought their way out during the night to join 82nd Airborne Division. 440th Armored Field Artillery was also cut off but it headed north to Vielsalm and drove through the German

## The Allied Counteroffensive

*Soldiers frantically dig in as German artillery zeros in on their position. One man has already been killed and the barrage could be heralding the start of an enemy attack. (NARA 111-SC-199202)*

lines with guns blazing as it crossed the river. The first attempt to demolish the Vielsalm bridge failed and the second attempt only collapsed part of the structure. Although foot troops could still cross the river, 9th SS Panzer Division's armour could not cross.

After a difficult 24 hours, the St Vith salient was clear and hardly anyone had been left behind. Hasbrouck's troops had stalled LXVI Corps for five days and limited the movement of both Sixth Panzer and Fifth Panzer Armies. They had also given XVIII Airborne Corps time to arrange a defensive line. In doing so Hasbrouck's command had suffered 4,000 casualties and lost over 100 tanks and armoured cars. But 15,000 men and 100 tanks had escaped and would turn around to fight again.

### Blunting Fifth Panzer Army's Advance

During the morning of 21 December the sound of armour approaching Hotton caused alarm in General Rose's headquarters. Part of 116th Panzer Division had slipped through CCR, 3rd Armored Division's positions and Kampfgruppe Bayer was aiming to get across the River Ourthe. Only 3rd Armored Division's command post and a few rear area units stood in its way but as the attack developed, General Rose ordered the part of CCR in Soy to attack Bayer's troops in the rear. The plan worked and Bayer's Kampfgruppe withdrew to wait for reinforcements; they never came but a battalion of 517th Parachute Regiment did reinforce Soy. Waldenburg eventually recalled Bayer's kampfgruppe at dusk due to a new development to the south.

The rest of LVIII Panzer Corps only made slow progress against CCR, 3rd Armored Division, while 560th VG Division spent all day trying to drive Task Force Orr back to Amonines. On the corps' left flank, 116th Panzer Division eventually drove Task Force Hogan out of La Roche but they dug in along the east bank of the Ourthe rather than surrender after they found their escape route blocked.

The seizure of La Roche gave 116th Panzer Division a bridge over the Ourthe and Waldenburg changed his plans to take advantage of it. During the night 560th VG Division took over the Hotton area while Kampfgruppe Bayer followed the rest of 116th Panzer Division across the river. 2nd Panzer Division had also crossed the Ourthe at Ortheuville, and it was heading for Marche alongside Panzer Lehr Division. Although the three divisions were advancing side-by-side towards Namur and Huy on the Meuse, Manteuffel was aware that casualties and tank losses were mounting. But his armour columns had to keep advancing whatever the cost.

The three panzer divisions were heading straight for VII Corps thin line and on 22 December General Collins ordered Rose to send

A battalion of 517th Parachute Regiment made the first counterattack against Hotton. Although it failed to push the Germans back, Pfc. Melvin Biddle bravely picked off German snipers and machine gun teams over a two-day period; he was awarded the Medal of Honor.

> Several attempts were made to air drop supplies to Task Force Hogan but they all failed. Instead, Rose's artillery units tried an innovative method to get essential items to the isolated men. Shell casings filled with medical supplies rather than explosives were fired into the perimeter.

part of CCA, 3rd Armored Division, to the Marche and St Hubert area to form a screen in front of them. Although the transfer left Rose short of troops, CCR, 3rd Armored Division, still fought 560th VG Division to a standstill at Hotton.

Task Force Hogan remained behind the German lines and refused to surrender. Elsewhere CCR, 3rd Armored Division was holding its own and while Task Force Orr was forced back to Amonines, Task Force Kane stopped the German advance at Lamormenil on the River Aisne.

23 December was a stalemate in the Hotton area as 560th VG Division tried in vain to dislodge CCR, 3rd Armored Division. Rose's defence between Hoy and Manhay had forced LVIII Panzer Corps to redirect 116th Panzer Division onto another route, costing it two days; two days in which First US Army had moved reserves forward.

## Delaying Fifth Panzer Army's Right Flank

Task Force Kane welcomed the arrival of CCA, 3rd Armored Division, at Manhay, only to see part of if head west to Marche. VII Corps was also able to report that 84th Division was only a few hours away but it needed time to deploy. The problem was that 2nd SS Panzer Division had crossed the Ourthe at Houffalize and was heading north towards Manhay.

The hamlet of Baraque de Fraiture stands at a major crossroads on a high exposed plateau five miles southeast of Manhay. It is where the north-south road connecting Liège and Bastogne meets the

*Surrounded by weapons, boxes of ammunition and cans of rations, crews of the 54th Field Artillery Battalion keep a careful watch from their foxholes as they prepare to support 3rd Armored Division's attack west of Houffalize. (NARA 111-SC-199254)*

east-west road running between St Vith and La Roche; both roads were important to Fifth Panzer Army. Major Arthur C. Parker III's three 105-mm howitzers of 589th Field Artillery Battalion were stationed at the crossroads on 20 December and they were joined by four half-tracks armed with multiple .50-calibre machine guns. After forming a tiny perimeter around the crossroads they waited to see who would arrive first.

On the morning of the 21st a German patrol was cut to pieces when it approached the crossroads and the alarm was sounded again when the engines were heard through the fog, only this time they belonged to 87th Cavalry Squadron. When the fog lifted late in the afternoon German reconnaissance vehicles could be seen in the distance; they belonged to 2nd SS Panzer Division.

General Rose, 3rd Armored Division's commander, summed up the grim situation on the Hotton to Manhay front for one of his subordinates: 'Impress on every individual that we must stay right here or there will be a war to be fought all over again, and we won't be here to fight it.'

As daylight faded Task Force Kane arrived with instructions to 'Hold as long as you can' but it was soon ordered to block another road. However, the garrison were pleased to welcome a company from 325th Glider Infantry that had dug in around Fraiture, only ½ mile to the northeast. All Parker's men could do now was to wait for the attack to start but the crossroads was only shelled; 2nd SS Panzer Division was waiting for fresh fuel supplies to arrive.

The attack began on the morning of 23 December and although the first attempt failed to dislodge Parker's men, 4th Panzer Grenadier Regiment and two tank companies overran the tiny garrison in the afternoon. Only 44 men (of 116 men) and three tanks escaped under cover of darkness. They had stalled 2nd SS Panzer Division's advance for a vital day, giving time for more troops to reach Manhay. Task Force Brewster also formed a new roadblock right in front of 2nd SS Panzer Division.

General Collins and VII Corps took over responsibility for the area during the night and while 560th VG Division had been stopped at Hotton, could 2nd SS Panzer Division be stopped at Manhay?

## Fifth Panzer Army Closes in on the Meuse

After a day waiting for fuel in front of Marche, 2nd Panzer Division's armour crept forward on 22 December, probing VII Corps outposts rather than making a full scale attack as Lüttwitz wanted. The timidity of the attack convinced Collins that XLVII Panzer Corps was hoping to outflank VII Corps and he ordered 84th Division to extend its positions southwest through Rochefort. News that the

*Young soldiers, both American and German, fought in appalling conditions, killing when necessary, to survive. Private Frank Vukasin loads a new clip into his rifle next to the bodies of two Germans during the fierce fighting around Rochefort. (NARA 111-SC-198859)*

British 29th Armoured Brigade had reached the Meuse at Namur, Dinant, and Givet was also a comfort; it meant the bridges were in safe hands.

2nd Panzer Division finally attacked 84th Division's line at Hargimont on 23 December but its advance was uncoordinated and when Lauchert called it off at dusk, Lüttwitz ordered him to keep the pressure on. 2nd Panzer Division reconnaissance units spent the night probing 84th Division's positions and by dawn they had broken through and advanced another eight miles to Leignon, leaving the rest of the division snaking back along the roads through Buissonville and Hargimont.

2nd Armored Division had reached the Marche area behind VII Corps lines on 23 December under a radio blackout and it was preparing to counterattack when news that German armour was as far north as Ciney caused alarm. Harmon ordered CCA, 2nd Armored Division, to investigate the sighting but after finding the village deserted, it regrouped, unaware that 2nd Panzer Division was only a short distance away.

Panzer Lehr Division had spent 22 December regrouping west of Bastogne while its reconnaissance troops checked the bridges over the Ourthe. It crossed the river around Moircy the following morning and drove through St Hubert, reaching Rochefort by dusk. Reconnaissance units reported that the town was unoccupied and Bayerlein gave the order to advance towards Dinant with the words, 'OK, let's go! Shut your eyes and go in!' His reconnaissance troops had been wrong and the armoured column was ambushed by 84th Division's small garrison as it drove into the town.

Fortunately for Bayerlein, his reconnaissance troops had found an unguarded bridge over the L'Homme River and part of his division slipped past Rochefort – or rather what was left of the division. By now Panzer Lehr Division had one kampfgruppe engaged at Bastogne, with a second kampfgruppe strung out forming roadblocks to guard Fifth Panzer Army's flank between Bastogne and Rochefort.

## The Battle for Bastogne Intensifies

While the rest of XLVII Panzer Corps headed west on 22 December, Lüttwitz ordered 26th VG Division to deal with Bastogne; and deal with it quickly. Panzer Lehr Division's probes had established that 101st Airborne Division's perimeter west of the town was disorganised and that is where he wanted to strike. The main attack fell on McAuliffe's battery positions between Villeroux and Mande-St Etienne and tanks from Team Pyle and Team Van Kleef fought alongside Team Browne's howitzers to stop it.

Although casualties were mounting, news that Third US Army was finally on the move to the south raised morale. McAuliffe's unusual response to a call to surrender also boosted the men's spirits. During the afternoon of the 22nd a party of German soldiers approached the American lines at Marvie under a white flag. They asked for the 'honourable surrender of the encircled town' promising 'annihilation' if the Americans refused.

> By this stage of the battle 101st Airborne Division's operations staff were getting concerned about Third US Army's progress and put out the following message: 'In regard to our situation, it is getting pretty sticky around here. They just keep coming. The enemy has attacked all along the south and some tanks are through and running around in our area. Request you inform 4th Armored Division of our situation and ask them to put on all possible pressure.'

McAuliffe struggled to compose an articulated reply and decided to give a one word answer; 'Nuts!' Colonel Joseph H. Harper, commander of 327th Glider Regiment, did not know how to translate the American slang word and instead told the Germans to go 'Go to Hell!' News of the surrender party's abrupt dismissal spread like wildfire around the perimeter.

The attacks against the Bastogne perimeter continued on 23 December as Panzer Lehr's kampfgruppe joined 26th VG Division's attack south of the town. The German artillery hammered the paratroopers' positions around Senonchamps, Marvie and Flamierge time after time, pausing only to let the infantry and tanks attack.

The only good news on 23 December was that the skies were clear allowing 241 cargo planes to drop over 140 tons of supplies, most of it artillery ammunition, on the drop zone west of the town. Then their P-47 fighter escorts attacked ground targets. The supply drops continued whenever the weather was clear, and on Christmas Day gliders loaded with surgeons and fuel landed inside the paratrooper's perimeter.

## Third US Army's Counterattack

Third US Army started its counterattack on 22 December once all its divisions were in position, as Eisenhower had asked for. III Corps

*C47 Dakota transport planes fly over Bastogne, dropping supplies; impossible early in the siege because of the weather. (NARA 111-SC-198403)*

had 80th Division on the right and 26th Division in the centre while 4th Armored Division was heading straight for Bastogne on its left flank. There was to be no artillery preparation and units were expected to move fast; General Patton had given all three divisional commanders the same order; 'Drive like hell'. 80th Division moved fast through Vichten, engaging 352nd VG Division as it moved through Ettelbrück. It continued north the following day, crossing the River Sure near Tadler and reached Kehmen having cut one of Seventh Army's main lines of communication. 80th Division had plenty of hard fighting ahead but it was stopping German reinforcements reaching the Bastogne area.

26th Division also advanced quickly until dusk, when it engaged Führer Grenadier Brigade and 352nd VG Division around Arsdorf. Patton wanted 26th Division to capture Wiltz, the home to Seventh Army headquarters, on 23 December but the advance towards the River Sure was slower than expected due to the number of inexperienced replacements the division had.

On III Corps' left, 4th Armored Division had to travel twelve miles to get to Bastogne and Patton told Gaffey to keep his task forces moving at all costs. In turn, Gaffey's orders to his subordinates; 'you

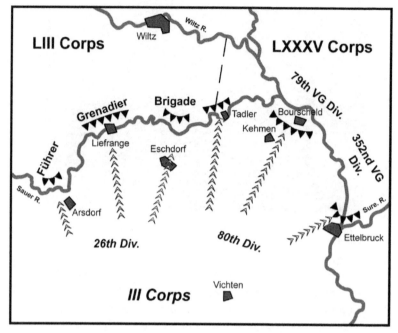

*III Corps advance towards Bastogne and the River Sure began on 22 December.*

will drive in, relieve the force, and proceed from Bastogne to the northeast …' It was a tall order because the division had to open a corridor into the town and cover III Corps' open left flank at the same time.

CCA, 4th Armored Division, advanced in two task forces parallel to the main Arlon-Bastogne road only to find a side road blocked by minefields and craters left by US engineers. Both task forces followed the main road north until they were stopped by a large crater at Martelange. German infantry then prevented the armoured infantry crossing the ruined bridge over the River Sure until late in the night. The engineers eventually bridged the river the following afternoon and although CCA was hoping to make up lost time, it ran into 5th Parachute Division's roadblocks

*GIs of the 10th Armored Infantry Battalion have left their halftracks behind as they advance across open fields during 4th Armored Division's advance towards Bastogne. (NARA 111-SC-199295)*

> Patton ordered Gaffey to move as fast as possible and the tanks, tank destroyers, self-propelled artillery and armoured engineers were formed into mobile columns. They would advance quickly, switching roads to bypass obstructions if necessary, to infiltrate deep into the German positions. The armoured infantry would follow in their halftracks, clearing up resistance in the villages.

at Warnach and the armour again had to wait for the armoured infantry to catch up.

CCB, 4th Armored Division, moved quickly along the secondary roads to the west of CCA until it ran into German positions around Burnon. It took until midnight to capture the village and bridge the stream running through it. It was stopped again in front of Chaumont on 23 December; it was only four miles from the Bastogne perimeter. As 4th Armored Division drove

> After a promising start, General Patton was becoming impatient with III Corps' progress and he told General Millikin to order his armour off the roads and to drive across the frozen fields to bypass the German roadblocks: 'There is too much piddling around. Bypass these towns and clear them up later. Tanks can operate on this ground now…' The commanders on the ground disagreed after watching their vehicles bog down in the thawing mud.

north, Seventh Army moved its spare armour against its open right flank during the night of 22 December and Major General Hugh J. Gaffey had to send forward the division's CCR to stop it breaking through. The Germans withdrew after a costly battle lasting 24 hours but Gaffey was also concerned that his division was running short of armour.

While III Corps made its drive towards Bastogne, XII Corps attacked Seventh Army, aiming to drive it back to the River Sauer. After six days of hard fighting, Barton's philosophy on combat rang true: 'The best way to handle these Heinies is to fight them.' The heroic defence of two US infantry regiments along the River Sauer had stopped three of Seventh Army's divisions breaking through. Partly this can be attributed to the German engineers' failure to quickly install bridges across the Sauer; but the dogged defence of several villages by the Americans had also stifled Seventh Army's advance.

LXXX Corps began preparing for the inevitable counterattack late on 21 December and 212th VG Division made a final attack on 22 December, covering its withdrawal to the River Sauer. Lieutenant General Manton S. Eddy's XII Corps took over the sector on the 23rd. 5th Division advanced and General Irwin noted that the 'situation on whole front from east of us to the north varies from fluid to no front at all. Information is very scanty and the situation changes hourly.'

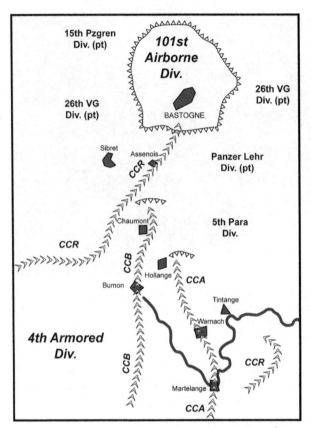

*4th Armored Division's advance towards Bastogne began on 22 December and CCR reached the paratroopers' perimeter on the 26th.*

## 24–25 December
## The Counteroffensive Intensifies

### Army Group B's Dilemma

Army Group B's advance was losing momentum by Christmas Eve but while Rundstedt was pessimistic about reaching the Meuse, Model ordered his generals to keep pushing. The Allies were not

*Treating casualties during the Battle of the Bulge was a logistical nightmare. These GIs of the 26th Division look around anxiously for a sniper, as one of their buddy's lies wounded on the cold ground during the attack on Wiltz. (NARA 111-SC-199092)*

having it all their own way either. Sixth Panzer Army was preparing to renew the attack on XVIII Airborne Corps following the fall of St Vith and while 9th SS Panzer Division crossed the Salm River at Vielsalm, 2nd SS Panzer Division had reached Salmchâteau and Manhay. West of the Ourthe, Fifth Panzer Army's advance was running out of steam but while 116th Panzer Division had been stopped in front of Marche, 2nd Panzer Division and Panzer Lehr Division were only a few miles from Dinant and the River Meuse.

While Army Group B's main hope lay with Fifth Panzer Army, the failure to capture Bastogne was absorbing a large number of troops and causing enormous problems on the congested road network. The failure of Seventh Army to keep up meant that Fifth Panzer Army's exposed south flank continued to expand. Manteuffel requested permission to regroup so that his troops could take Bastogne but his request was denied. Although Hitler had released part of OKW reserve, only one regimental combat team was sent to the Bastogne area. The Führer was determined to get across the Meuse and both 9th Panzer and 15th Panzer Grenadier Divisions were sent to support Fifth Panzer Army's advance.

## The Battle along the River Salm

By 24 December Sixth Panzer Army's advance was limited to the area west of the Salm River. Hitler had called off further attacks against V Corps positions and dropped the idea of using Fifteenth Army to extend the fighting north; LXVII Corps had also been stripped of armour. A final attack on Elsenborn Ridge on 28 December failed completely.

There was still only a thin line of American units between the Salm and Ourthe Rivers and Hodges had split the area between XVIII Airborne Corps and VII Corps on 23 December. 82nd Airborne

*Paratroopers of the 82nd Airborne Division dig foxholes and shelters on a hillside near Vaux Chavanne. The airborne soldiers performed admirably in their ground role and stopped II SS Panzer Corps' advance towards the Meuse. (NARA 111-SC-198422)*

Division held XVIII Airborne Corps' sector between Manhay, Vielsalm and Trois Ponts. Ridgway had also just taken over the 15,000 men and 100 tanks who had recently escaped from St Vith; while the armour and artillery reinforced Gavin's paratroopers, the foot soldiers formed a reserve.

9th SS Panzer Division spearheaded I SS Panzer Corps' attack from Vielsalm but a single platoon of paratroopers stopped the armour crossing the River Salm for some time. The rearguard action allowed 82nd Airborne Division to withdraw unmolested to a straighter, shorter line between Manhay and Trois Ponts.

9th Panzer Division eventually attacked 508th Parachute Regiment on 25 December but time after time it was stopped in its tracks. It withdrew after three days hard fighting having run short of armour, ammunition and fuel; Sixth Panzer Army's attacks were at an end and Dietrich knew that the Allied counteroffensive would start soon.

## The Battle for Manhay

75th Division was on its way to reinforce 3rd Armored Division between Hotton and Manhay and General Collins wanted it to counterattack as soon as it reached the area. II SS Panzer Corps aimed to break VII Corps line around Manhay before it was ready. 2nd SS Panzer Division advanced north towards Manhay, running into Task Force Brewster. Its armour soon ground to a halt due to the muddy conditions and its panzer grenadiers were unable to make any headway.

To the east, Führer Begleit Brigade had crossed the Salm at Salmchâteau but it too could not break 325th Glider Infantry Regiment's lines around Fraiture and Regne.

Ridgway ordered a reorganisation of his lines on the night of 24 December so that 82nd Airborne Division could form a shorter defensive line. However, the paratroopers began withdrawing from Manhay before CCA, 7th Armored Division, had taken over, following a misunderstanding. At the same time 2nd SS Panzer

*A 105mm howitzer shells German positions from beneath its camouflage netting under a darkening sky. (NARA 111-SC-197357)*

Division's tanks advanced using a timber road their engineers had built and took Grandmenil. They then followed a captured Sherman tank, fooling the American roadblocks into thinking they were friendly troops, and drove into Manhay just as the paratroopers were leaving. The mistake left Manhay in II SS Panzer Corps' hands, seriously compromising Ridgway's counterattack plan.

75th Division joined CCA, 7th Armored Division, on Christmas Day and they spent the day digging in north of Manhay, knowing that they were the last line of defence before the Meuse. They were unaware that 2nd SS Panzer Division had new orders to turn west and advance through Erezée, expecting to roll up VII Corps' line. Although II SS Panzer Corps was hoping to reach Huy on the Meuse, 2nd SS Panzer Division was stopped at Grandmenil on 25 December, having advanced less than a mile.

560th VG Division continued its attacks along the Aisne valley on 24 December but it was still unable to break Task Force Orr at Amonines or Task Force Kane at Freyneux and Lamormenil. Task Force Hogan also escaped on foot back to Hotton on Christmas Day.

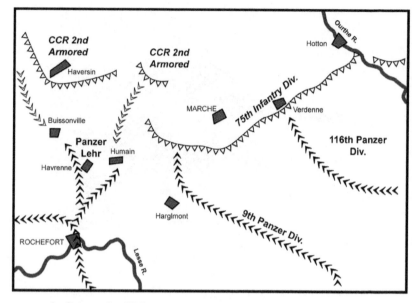

*By Christmas Day VII Corps had stopped LVIII Panzer Corps around Marche.*

## Fifth Panzer Army's Last Drive for the Meuse

Rundstedt was putting all his faith in Manteuffel and he told him to keep Fifth Panzer Army moving towards the Meuse, even if supply failures forced his men 'to proceed on foot'. While 12th SS Panzer Division and 3rd Panzer Grenadier Division had been earmarked to reinforce the attack, they were still some distance away and unlikely to affect the outcome of the battle in front of Dinant.

Montgomery and Hodges had wanted VII Corps to counterattack through the Rochefort area on 24 December but 2nd Armored Division was still deploying at dawn while 84th Division was strung out along a fifteen-mile front with LVIII Panzer Corps and XLVII Panzer Corps bearing down on it. As much as Collins would have liked to attack, the plan was postponed.

Instead 116th Panzer Division attacked VII Corps line east of Marche but a shortage of fuel limited the number of available vehicles and it could only secure a small lodgement in 84th Division's line at Verdenne. The lodgement was then cut off and nearly 300 Germans surrendered on Christmas Day. Some groups remained hidden in the woods, hoping that the Führer Begleit Brigade would reinforce them.

On VII Corps' opposite flank, the tiny Rochefort garrison stopped Panzer Lehr Division advancing for a crucial 24 hours and it finally made a break for freedom during the night. 2nd Armored Division was supposed to have reinforced the garrison but CCA's two task forces ran straight into German roadblocks between Buissonville and Celles; they cut 2nd Panzer Division's line of communications.

If that news was a surprise, General Harmon then heard that 2nd Panzer Division's leading kampfgruppe had reached Celles, meaning it was only four miles from Dinant. Although British troops were blocking the roads into the town, XLVIII Panzer Corps was nearly in sight of the Meuse. Harmon immediately alerted CCB, 2nd Armored Division and ordered it to prepare to counterattack the following morning.

While Fifth Panzer Army's situation map showed that XLVII Panzer Corps had three panzer divisions within reach of the Meuse at

*As a blizzard sets in GIs fight the elements to erect a barbed wire fence. Snow, rain, ice and mud were common enemies during the fighting in the Ardennes. (NARA 111-SC-198182)*

Dinant on Christmas Day, it did not show the true position on the ground.

Part of 2nd Panzer Division had been cut off while the Panzer Lehr Division only had a third of its strength at the tip of the salient. 9th Panzer Division had just taken over the line facing Marche and while it had orders to attack Buissonville, its artillery was stuck in traffic and it would be for several days. So while XLVII Panzer Corps' situation looked good on Army Group B's operations map, the situation on the ground was turning into a nightmare for Lüttwitz.

On Christmas Day CCA, 2nd Armored Division, counterattacked and ran straight into Panzer Lehr Division as it moved through Havrenne into Buissonville and Humain. CCA was able to take Havrenne but 4th Cavalry Group could not retake Humain.

2nd Panzer Division was supposed to advance into Dinant, but its reconnaissance troops were trapped around Foy-Notre-Dame while the leading kampfgruppe was stuck in woods between Celles and Conjoux.

As Lauchert prepared to renew the advance, CCB, 2nd Armored Division, struck. Task Force A rolled through Achêne, past the north side of the main group while Task Force B drove through Le Houisse and Conjoux to the east.

The Germans dared not counter the pincer move due to the large number of Allied planes circling overhead. CCB's two task forces met at Celles in the afternoon, trapping Lauchert's men in what became known as the 'Celles Pocket', and then watched while the fighter bombers strafed the woods. CCB's ring of tanks stopped the rest of 2nd Panzer Division breaking through and by nightfall it was obvious that the woods were a death trap. While 600 men abandoned their vehicles and escaped on foot during the hours of darkness, the rest were hunted down until the 'Celles Pocket' was clear.

## The Desperate Fight for Bastogne Continues

While Fifth Panzer Army was stalled in sight of the Meuse, Manteuffel still had the huge problem of Bastogne to deal with. As 26th VG

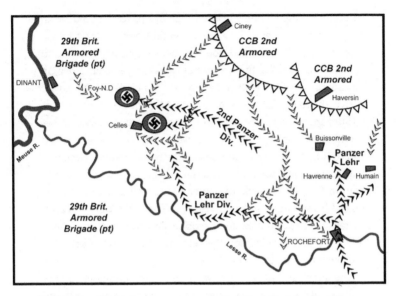

*XLVII Panzer Corps advance comes to a halt within sight of the River Meuse on Christmas Day.*

Division and Panzer Lehr's kampfgruppe probed their way around 101st Airborne's perimeter they discovered what McAuliffe already knew. The strength of the line of outposts had been irregular and the Germans were finding the weak points. On 24 December the paratroopers were reorganised into four equal reinforced combined arms teams to counter the problem and they built roadblocks on every road. While Colonel Roberts spread the available armour evenly around the perimeter, Team SNAFU and four tank destroyers deployed around the divisional headquarters in case McAuliffe's staff had to make a last stand. As the paratroops dug in they were wondering how they were going to get out of their predicament. McAuliffe was probably thinking the same when a message arrived from Third US Army's headquarter; it said 'Christmas Eve present coming up. Hold on.'

Manteuffel did not call a Christmas Day truce and 15th Panzer Grenadier Division's kampfgruppe was ordered to attack the northwest side of the perimeter at dawn, so it could be in Bastogne before the US Air Force fighter-bombers took to the skies. Colonel Maucke had objected because he had no time to prepare his men for the attack but he was overruled. Early on Christmas morning eighteen Panzer IV tanks loaded with soldiers drove through 327th Glider Regiment's lines at the head of 115th Panzer Grenadier Regiment's attack. The tanks drove across the frozen fields west of Champs, avoiding the roadblocks, rolled past the battalion command post and into the battery positions. Half turned west towards Mande-St Etienne where they clashed with Team Roberts while the other half turned east and ran into 502nd Parachute Regiment's reserves. The tanks were engaged by tank destroyers, tanks and bazookas and none returned. After a fierce battle for Champs, the rest of 115th Panzer Grenadier Regiment fell back to its own lines.

The attack against the southwest side of the perimeter on the morning of the 26th was stopped by the howitzer batteries massed

*These halftracks have been covered with white paint to try and make them blend in with a fresh fall of snow. Men huddle for warmth beneath a thin ground sheet as they wait for new orders inside their vehicles. (NARA 111-SC-199347)*

> During the siege the paratroopers had outnumbered the Germans troops gathered outside the perimeter since Lüttwitz's panzer divisions had headed west. However, while McAuliffe had to man the whole fifteen-mile perimeter around the clock, the Germans could choose where and when they wanted to attack.

on the outskirts of town. It would be one of the final attacks against the Bastogne perimeter due to important developments to the south.

## Third US Army Continues its Counterattack

Between 24 and 26 December 80th Division was involved in a bitter battle with 352nd VG Division in the forests, ravines and ridges around Ettelbrück. Major General Horace L. McBride's men persevered and once they reached the Sure to the east and the Sauer to the north, 352nd VG Division was forced to evacuate its bridgehead at Ettelbrück. Although the 80th could not eliminate the German bridgehead at Bourscheid, it could be proud of the fact that it had stopped two German infantry divisions and a panzer brigade reaching the Bastogne area.

Plans for 26th Division to capture Wiltz were thwarted when 79th VG Division and the Führer Grenadier Brigade drove a wedge between 26th Division and 80th Division. Task Force Hamilton entered Eschdorf on 24 December but it took two days to clear the village, giving the German engineers time to demolish the bridge over the Sure. The bridge at Liefrange was also destroyed and it took until the 26th to cross over the Sure near Arsdorf. Führer Grenadier Brigade then withdrew to the north bank and although a Bailey bridge was open for traffic on 27 December, it had taken three days for General Paul's men to get across the river; far too long for Patton's liking.

One of 80th Division's battalions spent all day fighting around Chaumont, alongside CCB. When two machine guns pinned down a platoon of 2/318th Regiment in Chaumont woods, Sergeant Paul J. Wiedorfer ran forward through the deep snow under fire to get them. He killed the first crew and captured the second allowing the advance to continue; he was awarded the Medal of Honor.

4th Armored Division was still meeting strong resistance on the road to Bastogne and it was unable to fulfil Patton's promise to reach the paratroopers on Christmas Eve. CCA advanced through Tintange and Hollange to bypass 5th Parachute Division's roadblocks along the main Bastogne-Arlon road but its progress was still too slow for Patton. General Gaffey needed extra foot troops to hold onto the ground his tanks had taken and 80th Division sent two battalions across to help.

The Germans withdrew from Chaumont and by nightfall CCB was at Hompre, only two miles from 101st Airborne Division's perimeter. CCR had also switched to 4th Armored Division's left flank and on Christmas Day it advanced rapidly from Bercheux to Remonville, coming up alongside CCB, widening 4th Armored Division's front. During the night 1st Lieutenant Walter P. Carr led a foot patrol into the Bastogne perimeter and he returned to Gaffey with a situation map showing the paratroopers' positions.

On the west bank of the Sauer, XII Corps 5th Division and 10th Armored Division aimed to establish bridgeheads across the river on 24 December. Both of LXXX Corps divisions were weary after a week of heavy fighting and although Kniess's troops were in good defensive country, they had the river to their backs and few bridges to escape across.

10th Armored Division attacked 276th VG Division on 24 December and while Task Force Standish cleared the area west

*Private Lloyd Spence and Private James Bryson pause for a few moments during 26th Division's counterattack. Having taken Arsdorf on Christmas Day the 'Yankee' Division regrouped and advanced towards Wiltz. (NARA 111-SC-198161)*

of Eppeldorf, Task Force Rudder took Gilsdorf on the riverbank. 5th Division also captured Hill 313 overlooking the Echternach bridgehead. The German evacuation of the Schwarz Erntz gorge marked the start of a general withdrawal towards the river. While 10th Armored Division spent Christmas Day reorganising, 5th Division continued advancing towards the river either side of Echternach.

# 26 December Onwards
# Driving Army Group B Back

## Revised Plans for SHAEF and Army Group B

Bradley visited 21st Army Group's headquarters on 25 December to ask Montgomery for an early counterattack but the Field Marshal was still concerned that Fifth Panzer Army or Sixth Panzer Army could break through First US Army's lines. Eisenhower had been more concerned about Third US Army's lack of progress towards Bastogne but now that 4th Armored Division was close to the paratroopers' perimeter, it was time to consider how to reduce Army Group B's huge salient.

Patton wanted his Third US Army to attack immediately northeast from the Bastogne area, cutting off Fifth Panzer Army's salient at its base; Eisenhower believed his plan was too ambitious. Montgomery wanted to attack southeast from Celles, driving back the nose of Fifth Panzer Army's salient; Eisenhower considered his plan was too cautious. Possible bad weather, the poor road network and a shortage of reserves led him to come up with a compromise. Third US Army would attack north from Bastogne on 30 December, drawing German reserves towards it. First US Army Corps would then attack south from Malmédy on 3 January and the two would meet between Houffalize and St Vith.

Model had also revised his plans and while Fifth Panzer and Sixth Panzer Armies had to destroy the Allied forces east of the Meuse, Seventh Army would stay on the defensive. While the plan was acceptable to Hitler, it was far too ambitious for the troops available on the ground. Model and Rundstedt agreed that the newly formed *Army Group Lüttwitz* had to take Bastogne and on 29 December Manteuffel told his commanders that the Ardennes offensive was over. Instead the immediate objective was to take Bastogne. But first they had to cut the corridor south of the town and XXXIX Corps would attack first from the east while XLVII Panzer Corps would follow with an attack from the west.

## II SS Panzer Corps Stopped around Manhay

2nd SS Panzer Division made one final attempt to advance north of Manhay and west of Erezée on 26 December but it was too weak to break the American line. XVIII Airborne Corps counterattacked on 27 December and while Task Force McGeorge recaptured Grandmenil, 7th Armored Division troops entered Manhay during the night, finding that 2nd SS Panzer Division had abandoned it. 9th SS Panzer Division took over the sector soon afterwards, but it was too late to make a difference.

There was one final opportunity when VII Corps reorganised its line during the night of 27 December, resulting in a large gap opening between Grandmenil and Erezée. 12th SS Panzer Division had just reached the area and two of its panzer grenadier companies slipped through 75th Division's line around Sadzot hamlet. One of 82nd Airborne's parachute battalions was ambushed when it moved forward to block the German penetration and it took over 24 hours of hard fighting before the panzer grenadiers were forced to surrender.

The incident became known as the 'Sad Sack Affair' and it marked the end of Sixth Panzer Army's offensive. Dietrich was ordered to

*The crunch of fresh snow is almost audible as this GI watches intently for signs of the enemy while clutching his BAR automatic weapon. (NARA 111-SC-199107)*

go over to the defensive and while there was talk of renewing the offensive, the men were too tired, units were too disorganised and supplies were too low.

## Counterattack around Marche

Fifth Panzer Army's attempt to reach the Meuse was also at an end. Throughout 26 December 84th Division's artillery and mortars hammered 116th Panzer Division's isolated position at Verdenne and Waldenburg ordered his troops to withdraw during the night and dig in to await the inevitable American counterattack.

9th Panzer Division moved troops into Humain and Rochefort on 26 December, allowing Panzer Lehr Division to advance towards the Celles Pocket. Bayerlein had hoped to reach the trapped part of 2nd Panzer Division but his troops were unable to break through CCB, 2nd Armored Division. They found themselves in danger the following day when CCA, 2nd Armored Division, counterattacked. As CCA's advance gained momentum, Harmon gave the task forces permission 'go to the River Lesse with abandon', trapping Panzer Lehr Division and stopping 9th Panzer Division breaking out.

At the same time CCR, 2nd Armored Division, forced 9th Panzer Division to withdraw from Humain and US Air Force fighter bombers targeted Elverfeldt's armoured columns when they tried to retake the village; XVLVII Corps's advance was at an end. On 28 December 83rd Division and British 53rd Division relieved 2nd Armored Division, blocking all the roads to the Meuse. Fifth Panzer Army had been so close to reaching the river but from now on it would be on the defensive.

## The Battle for the Bastogne Corridor

Manteuffel also had to focus on the developing situation south of Bastogne as well as the problems at the tip of Fifth Panzer Army's salient. CCR, 4th Armored Division, kept pushing towards the town

> S/Sergeant James R. Hendrix's half-track came under fire during the battle for Assenois so he dismounted and single-handedly captured two 88mm guns and their crews. He dismounted a second time to provide covering fire as two wounded soldiers were rescued and a third time to free an injured man from a burning half-track. Hendrix was awarded the Medal of Honor.

on 26 December, and it was about to attack Sibret when there was last minute change of plan. Lieutenant Colonel Creighton W. Abrams Jr. wondered if a task force could drive quickly through the German roadblocks in Assenois and reach the paratroopers' lines. His idea became a plan and the order was passed down the chain of command until Captain William A. Dwight told his subordinate officers; 'It's the push!'

While artillery provided covering fire, the small task force of tanks and halftracks loaded with infantry headed north. They came under fire in Assenois and while the infantry dismounted to engage the enemy, the tanks kept moving only to run into another German ambush. Lieutenant Charles P. Boggess ordered his unit of five Sherman tanks and one half-track forward to help Dwight and before long the tanks were moving again. At around 16:45 hours men of the 326th Airborne Engineer Battalion saw 'three light tanks believed friendly' approaching their outposts; it was Boggess' group and Task Force Dwight was close behind. Twenty minutes later Colonel Abrams was shaking hands with General McAuliffe at the outpost line. The relief of Bastogne had begun.

The rest of CCR cleared the Assenois area during the night, taking over 500 prisoners, and by the early hours of 27 December light tanks were escorting 40 supply trucks and 70 ambulances into Bastogne. There had been over 2,000 casualties inside the perimeter during the week-long siege and many of the wounded had waited days to be evacuated. CCR, 4th Armored Division, escorted

*Medics carry their wounded through the snow to the aid stations. These men were wounded during 35th Division's attempt to relieve Bastogne. The 'Sante Fe' Division held off four German divisions and captured Villers-la Bonne-Eau, a battle that lasted thirteen days. (NARA 111-SC-199234)*

many convoys along the road between Assenois and Bastogne during the day, taking supplies in and bringing over 950 wounded and 700 prisoners out. General Taylor also entered the town and congratulated McAuliffe when he resumed command of the 101st Airborne.

4th Armored Division's breakthrough surprised the German troops on the ground and at Fifth Panzer Army headquarters. 26th VG Division and 5th Parachute Division now had to stop 4th Armored Division widening its corridor into Bastogne while maintaining pressure on the paratroopers' perimeter around the town. Manteuffel only had Führer Begleit Brigade spare to counterattack and although reinforcements were being sent towards Bastogne, they would take time to reach the area.

While 4th Armored Division secured the neck of the corridor, 35th Division joined the fight between Surre and Livarchamps, on its right flank. CCA, 9th Armored Division also tried to widen the west side of the corridor on 27th but 26th VG Division was determined not to let it. While Task Force Collins fought for Sibret and Chenogne, Task Force Karsteter attacked Villeroux and Senonchamps; in both cases the American armour won the battle. Führer Begleit Brigade and the remaining tanks of 3rd Panzer Grenadier Division also joined the battle but CCA had already doubled the size of the corridor.

## Third Army's Counterattacks Either Side of Bastogne

Snow and sleet swept across the Ardennes as control of the Bastogne area was handed back to VIII Corps. Third US Army's plan was for 101st Airborne Division to hold the town while 6th Armored Division attacked from the east side of the town; but General Grow's armour had to pass along congested roads to get through 4th Armored Division. At the same time CCA,

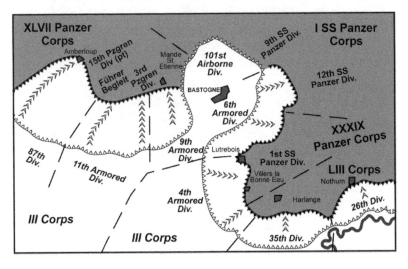

*Third Army's 30 December attack met strong resistance from Army Group Lüttwitz either side of Bastogne but by 2 January Fifth Panzer Army had been forced away from the town.*

9th Armored Division, 11th Armored Division and 87th Division would advance west of the town. The plan was them to push north towards Houffalize, cutting into the base of Fifth Panzer Army's salient.

Third US Army's counterattack began on 30 December and 87th Division attacked Panzer Lehr Division between St Hubert and the River Ourthe on the west flank. Major General Frank L. Culin's troops met heavy resistance and they took three days to get through Moiry and Amberloup, before they reach their initial objective, the main road west of Bastogne. 11th Armored Division had only just reached the Continent and it went into action after a difficult night march. CCB's Task Force Pat advanced up the Rechrival valley in the centre but Führer Begleit Brigade stopped Task Force Poker taking Chenogne. CCA was stopped at Remagne, so it joined CCB's advance. CCA, 9th Armored Division eventually drove 3rd Panzer Grenadier Division out of Chenogne and Senonchamps on 11th Armored Division's right flank.

Führer Begleit Brigade counterattacked Task Force Pat the following morning and it only withdrew from the Rechrival valley after a vicious battle. Task Force Poker kept attacking, capturing Mande-St Etienne on 2 January. 17th Airborne Division took over 11th Armored Division's sector the following day.

As 6th Armored Division moved into Bastogne, Third US Army did not know that I SS Panzer Corps had joined Army Group *Lüttwitz*. As General Grow's armour squeezed past 4th Armored Division,

It had been a brutal first battle for Major General Charles S. Kilburn's men. In four days 11th Armored Division suffered 750 casualties and lost over sixty tanks. An advance of six miles in three days was hardly the big push Patton was hoping for but 11th Armored Division had stopped XLVII Panzer Corps cutting the Bastogne corridor.

*Tanks and halftracks of the 6th Armored Division battle with 12th SS Panzer Division east of Bastogne. (NARA 111-SC-198856)*

1st SS Panzer Division and 12th SS Panzer Division were heading towards the east side of Bastogne, while 9th SS Panzer Division was moving towards the north side of the town.

CCA, 6th Armored Division advanced on time on 30 December but it did not advance far past Neffe; CCB's advance was delayed by a day due to the traffic congestion and it failed to take Arloncourt. As 6th Armored Division prepared to attack on 2 January, Army Group *Lüttwitz* struck back. CCA had a confused battle around Wardin, one in which American troops fired on each other, while CCB ran into 12th SS Panzer Division and 167th VG Division. Although Grow's division had captured ground east of Bastogne, it was running out of armour and could not go much further. Yet again Patton's hopes for a rapid advance had been dashed.

While XVLII Panzer Corps' western pincer against the Bastogne corridor had stopped, XXXIX Corps went ahead with attacking the eastern side on 31 December. 35th Division fought 1st SS Panzer Division to a standstill around Lutrebois over the next three days; the battles for Villers-la-Bonne-Eau and Harlange woods lasted much longer. On III Corps' right wing 26th Division advanced alone across the River Sure on 27 December, looking to capture Wiltz, but it was unable to take Kaundorf and the highest hill in the area. It cut the Wiltz road the following afternoon but it had not taken Wiltz village.

## XII Corps along the River Sauer

By 26 December LXXX Corps was only holding two small bridgeheads on the west bank of the River Sauer. One by one the German positions were cleared and a general withdrawal began when the American troops seized the high ground overlooking the river. The US artillery could then shell the queues of German assault guns and vehicles waiting to cross the Sauer bridges; many men were forced to swim the freezing river to escape.

General Patton had no intentions of crossing the Sauer and 5th, 80th and 4th Infantry Divisions were ordered to dig in along the west bank while their supporting armour was moved towards Bastogne. XII Corps front would remain quiet until the advance towards the West Wall began in earnest on 18 January.

## Army Group B on the Defensive

Sixth Panzer and Fifth Panzer Armies attempts to reach the Meuse were over and their troops were on the defensive all around the salient, exactly as Model had warned. But it was not the end of the fighting in the Ardennes; Eisenhower wanted to erase the Bulge in the Allied line as quickly as possible.

The capture of Mande-St Etienne to the west of Bastogne on 2 January meant that III Corps was on course to trapping XLVII Panzer Corps' three weak divisions in the Rochefort salient. 26th Division's advance southeast of the town was also cutting across XXXIX Corps' rear, threatening to trap several divisions. Seventh Army's sector south of Bastogne was particularly in danger but Model refused when Brandenberger asked for permission to withdraw 5th Parachute Division from the 'Harlange Pocket'.

> Despite the shortage of infantry reinforcements, Afro-Caribbean troops could only serve in service units; 250,000 were working along the lines of communication. Many responded to the call for combat volunteers but the battle was over by the time they were trained. 4,500 eventually served in segregated companies.

Manteuffel knew that the sensible option was to withdraw Fifth Panzer Army to a shorter line running north to south between Vielsalm, Houffalize and Bastogne. He could then select a good defensive line and withdraw units into a reserve. While it was a realistic plan, agreed in principle by Model, the Führer would not allow it. Instead, Army Group B had to persist with plans to take Bastogne. Even though Rundstedt and Model knew that the Allies would be aiming to erase the Bulge as quickly as possible, they were both powerless to act against Hitler's wishes.

## Operation *Nordwind*

While the Battle in the Ardennes drew to a close, another German offensive, Operation *Nordwind*, was launched in Northern Alsace. At the same time as Operation *Wacht am Rhein* began on 16 December, General Hermann Balck of Army Group G was warned to prepare to attack Seventh US Army starting with First Army advancing either side of Bitche into the Saverne Gap. Operation *Nordwind* got the go ahead on 22 December the same day that General Johannes Blaskowitz took over Army Group G.

On the evening of 31 December three corps attacked, XIII SS Corps on the right flank, LXXXX in the centre and LXXXIX Corps on the left. It seems that Seventh US Army did not know of the impending attack but the initial breakthroughs had been contained by the end of the second day. The advance was over by the end of the third and most of First Army's troops were back on the start line.

# THE LEGACY

## Eliminating the Bulge

SHAEF was running out of American reinforcements by the turn of the New Year but Eisenhower was anxious to strike back before Fifth Panzer Army withdrew from the Bulge. Third US Army was pushing hard on both sides of Bastogne, but Manteuffel was not going to give in without a fight and he moved all his available troops towards the town to stop Patton's advance. While VIII Corps engaged the bulk of Fifth Panzer Army, III Corps advanced north east, aiming to cut off its escape route.

On New Year's Day 1945 the Luftwaffe launched Operation *Baseplate (Bodenplatte)*, a wave of air attacks to wipe out Allied air superiority over the Ardennes. Over 1,000 planes struck airfields across northern Europe and although 300 Allied planes were destroyed, 230 German pilots and many planes were lost in the attack. While the Allies could replace their losses, Hermann Göring's Luftwaffe could not.

*116th Panzer Division drove through a deserted Houffalize on 19 December as it headed west. On 16 January, 2nd and 11th Armored Division entered the town after a two week battle, connecting First and Third US Armies attacks. (NARA 111-SC-199256)*

First US Army also launched its attack on the north side of the salient on 3 January and while VII Corps led the advance towards Houffalize, XVIII Airborne Corps attacked Sixth Panzer Army alongside.

The Allies offensive suffered the same difficulties the Germans had experienced while advancing across rugged terrain in bad weather. Armour was limited to the few roads and it was often down to the infantry to battle it out alone. For two weeks the American troops advanced village by village in appalling conditions until Fifth Panzer Army finally withdrew from the shrinking salient, allowing First and Third US Armies to meet in the ruins of Houffalize. The shortening of the line released American reserves and Eisenhower ordered a general advance eastwards to completely remove the Bulge.

## The Cost

By the middle of January 1945 the Bulge had been virtually erased and although there were times when it had seemed as though the

*With the counteroffensive underway thousands of prisoners began to flood in during the German withdrawal. Paratroopers of the 82nd Airborne Division took this well equipped soldier, complete with snowsuit, near Fosse. (NARA 111-SC-198552)*

Allies were in dire peril, Operation *Wacht am Rhein* had failed to achieve any of its objectives. It had only served to seriously reduce Germany's reserves, in men, material and supplies; all of them irreplaceable. The Wehrmacht would be on the defensive from now on and it would only be a matter of time until the Allies broke through the Siegfried Line, entered Germany and crossed the Rhine. Both armies had suffered terrible losses. Well over half a million Allied soldiers, the vast majority American, had fought Army Group B to a standstill and then pushed it back beyond its starting line. Over 40,000 American soldiers were killed or wounded stopping the advance, a similar number of casualties were reported in erasing the Bulge. The German losses are more difficult to ascertain but figures vary between 80,000 and 100,000 for both phases. What is certain is that the battle ended Germany's capacity to stage offensive operations. The Allies had weathered the worst storm Hitler could throw at them

## Analysing the Ardennes Battle

The initial success and ultimate failure of Operation *Wacht am Rhein* raises many questions. Army Group B had built up considerable strength in the Ardennes, particularly in armoured and mechanised divisions, without raising the Allies' suspicions. The attack had been a complete surprise and yet, looking back it is clear that it was bound to fail after only a few days. So what went wrong?

The problems caused by Hitler interfering in Army Group B's every move and the discrepancies in actual and reported orders of battle have already been discussed. The *Wacht am Rhein* timetable was also very ambitious, particularly when factors such as the poor road network and bad weather are taken into account. At times it seems as through the expected rate of advance ignored the possibility that American troops might try to defend key positions or might demolish bridges.

The Volks Grenadier Divisions took far longer than planned to break through and delayed the waiting panzer divisions. Most Volks Grenadier units did not perform as well as expected but it was hardly surprising, considering that the men were inexperienced and short of heavy weapons. It also took longer than expected to bridge the rivers running along large parts of the front line, compromising Fifth Panzer's advance over the Our and Seventh Army's advance across the Sauer. Army Group B's advance was behind schedule before it got underway due to the combination of the above factors.

By the end of the first day there were several ruptures in First US Army's line but the gaps were neither wide enough nor deep enough. The limited advance in the Elsenborn area would stifle Sixth Panzer Army's advance throughout the battle and while Kampfgruppe Peiper's advance set the standard, it was delayed due to the limited road network and then stopped and destroyed.

*A bugler of the 9th Armored Division sounds 'Taps' as the colour party stands to attention. The division was committed piecemeal to stem the German breakthrough and it was instrumental in preventing Fifth Panzer Army from seizing Bastogne. (NARA 111-SC-199411)*

2nd Panzer Division also broke through in Fifth Panzer Army's area but small task forces and a few engineers slowed its advance to a crawl. Seventh Army had too little armour and artillery to make a difference on the southern flank.

If Hitler had expected Army Group B to be at the Meuse in 48 hours, then it was seriously behind schedule by the end of the first day. Model expected it to be at the Meuse in four days, a target which was still achievable, but not for long. By the third day of the offensive, Sixth Panzer Army had been stopped and although Fifth Panzer Army's advance was gaining momentum, its inability to quickly take St Vith and Bastogne with their important road networks caused many problems. By day five Army Group B's offensive was out of control and turning into a series of haphazard improvisations. Third US Army began its counter offensive on day seven and from that point on, Model and his three army generals were reacting to American counterattacks.

Why had Army Group B's mass of armoured and mechanised troops failed to break out as planned? Firstly, the American defence line had been more stubborn than anticipated and many positions held out far longer than expected. Rapid rupture of the defensive positions was only achieved in a few places, such as the Schnee Eiffel, and it severely restricted Army Group B's advance.

The delay in front of St Vith delayed Fifth Panzer Army for several days while the failure to take Bastogne limited Manteuffel's lines of communications throughout the battle. The inability of Sixth Panzer Army and Seventh Army to keep pace on the flanks of the salient also adversely affected Fifth Panzer Army's advance.

SHAEF was quick to move reserves to the Ardennes, far quicker than Rundstedt or Model expected. They were also both surprised that SHAEF was prepared to strip so many troops from other sectors to reinforce the Ardennes. It revealed the flexibility in the Allied command, a flexibility that Hitler denied OKW and Army Group. Hitler and OKW were slow to release reserves and they were then delayed on the overloaded road network; by the time they reached the front line they were too late to make a difference to Army Group B's fortunes.

If doubts about the success of the offensive were creeping into Model's mind by 20 December, then they intensified four days later when the weather changed. As the Allied Air Forces took to the skies, Army Group B's northern flank was at a standstill, the tip of its salient had stalled and Third US Army was squeezing its southern flank. Only XLVII Panzer Corps was still moving forward even though its corps commander was recommending a withdrawal; his request was denied. Manteuffel was also sure that 'the objective could no longer be attained'.

The relief of Bastogne on 26 December shocked OB West and General Hans Krebs, Model's chief of staff, noted that 'Today a certain culminating point [has been reached]'. From then on the Americans had the initiative and while Army Group B was on the defensive, it was not allowed to withdraw. On 31 December OB WEST noted that if Bastogne could not be taken 'that is the end of the offensive operation'. Hitler had also lost interest in the Ardennes to focus on the Eastern Front; but Army Group B still had a hard fight in front of it as it struggled to contain the Allied counteroffensive throughout January 1945.

## The Place of the Ardennes Offensive in the Second World War

Nazi propagandists naturally claimed the Ardennes offensive had crippled the Allied attack capabilities; but Army Group B had suffered equally. While the Allies had the capability to replace men and material, Germany did not. The German attack in the Ardennes was the last Wehrmacht offensive of the Second World War; but there was another four months of hard fighting ahead of SHAEF before Nazi Germany capitulated.

Hitler's decision to stake everything on Wacht am Rhein would, if anything, shorten the war. Sending so many reinforcements to the Western Front, had left the Eastern Front short. By the end of December OKW was looking to the east where a huge Soviet offensive was threatened; it began on 12 January and by the beginning of February Russian troops were less than 50 miles from Berlin.

On 27 February 1945 Eisenhower sent the following cable to General George Marshall, the US Army's Chief of Staff based in Washington D.C.: 'I have seen press reports emanating from Washington and purporting to quote the War Department official to the effect that the Ardennes battle was the costliest in American history. I also suggest that it was one of the most profitable. The casualties over the Ardennes month averaged no more than for the two months before. The cost of material was actually very light. The main effect was a major catastrophe for the Germans.'

*As the number of German tanks dwindled, the weight of American armour begon to tell and the larger, slower tanks became prey to lighter and faster tank destroyers. The Allies would be able to replace their losses – the Wehrmacht would not. (NARA 111-SC-198889)*

Had Hitler's gamble been worth it? Hitler committed suicide in Berlin on 30 April 1945, as Soviet troops closed in on his Führer bunker. Field Marshals Jodl and Keitel were tried in Nuremberg, the trials beginning in October 1945 and were found guilty of war crimes and condemned to death a year later. They made a joint statement shortly before their execution: As to 'the criticism whether it would have been better to have employed our available reserves in the East rather than in the West, we submit to the judgment of history.' Having read this book, you can make your own judgement.

# ORDERS OF BATTLE

## Army Group B on 16 December 1944

**Sixth Panzer Army;**
Oberstgruppenführer der Waffen SS
Josef Dietrich

North Flank
**LXVII Corps;** Generalleutnant Otto
  Hitzfeld
*272nd Volks Grenadier Division;* General
  Major Eugen König
*326th Volks Grenadier Division;* Oberst
  Kosmalla

South Flank
**I SS Panzer Corps;** SS-Gruppenführer
  Hermann Priess
*1st SS Panzer Division;* SS-Oberführer
  Wilhelm Mohnke
*3rd Parachute Division;* General Major
  Wadehn
*12th SS Panzer Division;* SS Standartenführer
  Hugo Kraas
*12th Volks Grenadier Division;* General Major
  Gerhard Engel
*277th Volks Grenadier Division;* Oberst
  Wilhelm Viebig

*Panzer Brigade 150 (Brandenburger Brigade);*
  SS Obersturmbannführer Otto Skorzeny

Second Wave
**II SS Panzer Corps;** SS Obergruppenführer
  Willi Bittrich
*2nd SS Panzer Division;* SS Brigadeführer
  Heinz Lammerding
*9th SS Panzer Division;* SS Oberführer
  Sylvester Stadler

**Fifth Panzer Army; General der
Panzertruppen Hasso von Manteuffel**

North Flank
**LXVI Corps;** General der Artillerie Walter
  Lucht
*18th Volks Grenadier Division;* Oberst
  Hoffman-Schönborn
*62nd Volks Grenadier Division;* Oberst
  Frederich Kittel Centre
**LVIII Panzer Corps;** General der
  Panzertruppen Walter Krüger
*116th Panzer Division;* General Major
  Siegfried von Waldenburg

# Orders of Battle

*560th Volks Grenadier Division;* Oberst Rudolf Langhaeuser

South Flank

**XLVII Panzer Corps;** General der Panzertruppen Heinrich Freiherr von Lüttwitz

*2nd Panzer Division;* Oberst Meinrad von Lauchert

*Panzer Lehr Division;* Generalleutant Fritz Bayerlein

*26th Volks Grenadier Division;* Oberst Heinz Kokott

Second Wave

**XXXIX Panzer Corps;** Generalleutant Karl Decker

*Joined 20 December 9th Panzer Division;* General Major Harald Freiherr von Elverfeldt

*Joined 20 December 15th Panzergrenadier Division;* Oberst Hans Deckert

## Seventh Army; General der Panzertruppen Erich Brandenberger

North Flank

**LXXXV Corps;** General der Infantrerie Baptist Kniess

*5th Parachute Division;* Oberst Ludwig Heilmann

*352nd Volks Grenadier Division;* Oberst Erich Schmidt

Centre

**LXXX Corps;** General der Infanterie Franz Beyer

*212th Volks Grenadier Division;* General Major Franz Sensfuss

*276th Volks Grenadier Division;* General Major Kurt Möhring

South Flank

**LIII Corps;** General der Kavallerie Edwin von Rothkirch. A mixture of low-grade fortress troops and a punishment battalion

## Reserve Release Dates

Army Group B Reserve to Seventh Army on 22 December

*79th Volks Grenadier Division;* Oberst Alois Weber

Assigned from Fifteenth Army to Fifth Panzer Army

On 20 December *9th Panzer Division;* General Major Harald Freiherr von Elverfeldt

On 26 December *340th Volks Grenadier Division;* Oberst Theodor Tolsdorff

To Seventh Army on 20 December

*15th Panzergrenadier Division;* Oberst Hans Joachim Deckert

OKW Reserve to Sixth Panzer Army on 26 December

On 19 December *3rd Panzergrenadier Division;* General Major Walter Denkert

On 26 December *246th Volks Grenadier Division;* Oberst Peter Koerte

To Fifth Panzer Army

On 17 December *Führer Begleit Brigade;* Oberst Otto Remer

On 22 December *167th Volks Grenadier Division;* Generalleutant Hanskurt Höcker

To Seventh Army on 22 December

*Führer Grenadier Brigade;* Oberst Hans Joachim Kahler

*9th Volks Grenadier Division;* Oberst Werner Kolb

## Typical German Army Divisional Organisations

By this stage of the war, the German armaments industry and transportation system were being routinely bombed, disrupting production of everything from tanks to ammunition and from transport to lubricants. Units were often under strength before they went into battle and even slightly damaged vehicles had to be abandoned due to a lack of replacement parts. On the whole, SS units had priority, and they were equipped with superior tanks, the best equipment and were kept well supplied at the expense of others.

## Panzer Division

2 × Panzer Regiments with 2 × battalions
2 × PzGrenadier Regts with 2 × battalions
Panzer Artillery Regiment with 2 × battalions
Armoured Reconnaissance Battalion
Air Defence Battalion
Tank Hunter Battalion

Panzer Pioneer Battalion
Signals Battalion
Panzer Divisions were organised into flexible kampfgruppes, or battle groups, each with a mix of armour, panzergrenadiers and artillery suitable to take the objective.

## Panzer Grenadier Division

2 × Panzergrenadier Regiments with 3 battalions
1 × Panzer Battalion
Artillery Regiment with 3 × battalions
Armoured Reconnaissance Battalion
Tank Hunter Troop
Air Defence Battalion
Pioneer Battalion
Signals Battalion

## Volks Grenadier Division

3 × Grenadier-Regiments
Pioneer-Battalion
Artillery Regiment with 4 × battalions
Tank Hunter Battalion

## First Army on 16 December 1944

### V Corps; Major General Leonard T. Gerow

*99th Infantry Division;* Major General Walter E. Lauer; Monschau and Gerolstein Forests
*2nd Infantry Division;* Major General Walter M. Robertson; in the centre of 99th Division

### VIII Corps; Major General Troy H. Middleton

*14th Cavalry Group;* Colonel Mark A. Devine Jr.; Losheim Gap

*106th Infantry Division;* Major General Alan W. Jones; On the Schnee Eifel ridge
*28th Infantry Division;* Major General Norman D. Cota; Along the Our River
*9th Armored Division;* Major General John W. Leonard; A single combat command
*4th Infantry Division;* Major General Raymond O. Barton; Along the Sauer River

# Orders of Battle

## Typical US Army Divisional Organisations

### Infantry Division

3 Regiments each with 3 battalions
Reconnaissance Troop
Engineer Combat Battalion
Medical Battalion
3 x 105mm Field Artillery Battalions
1 x 155mm Field Artillery Battalion
Attached:
Up to three tank battalions
Mobile anti-aircraft battalion
Towed tank destroyer battalion
Mobile tank destroyer battalion
Heavy mortar battalion

### Airborne Division

3 x Parachute Regiments each with
3 battalions
1 x Glider Regiment with 1 battalion
Parachute Maintenance Battalion
Airborne Engineer Battalion
Airborne Medical Company
Airborne Antiaircraft Artillery Battalion
2 x Glider Field Artillery Battalions
2 x Parachute Field Artillery Battalion

### Armoured Division

3 Tank Battalions
3 Armoured Infantry Battalions
Cavalry Reconnaissance Squadron
Armoured Engineer Battalion
3 Armoured Field Artillery Battalions
Armoured Medical Battalion

US Armoured divisions were organised into three flexible combat commands. While Combat Commands A and B engaged the enemy, Combat Command R was held in reserve. Troops were allocated to Combat Commands A and B and the tanks and armoured infantry were formed into mixed combat groups to suit the terrain and the objective.

# VISITING THE BATTLEFIELD

A map of all the Battle of the Bulge sites and a brochure called The *Battle of the Ardennes: Down Memory Lane* can be bought at many of the museums in the area or by contacting the Belgium Tourism offices in the region of Wallonia. The Bastogne Tourist Office is situated in McAuliffe Square. One book dedicated to visiting the Ardennes is *A Tour of the Bulge Battlefield* by William Cavanagh (Pen and Sword, 2001).

The following list details the main museums in the Ardennes area.

Bastogne Historical Center, Bastogne:
http://www.bastognehistoricalcenter.be/
Ardennen Poteau '44 Museum, Poteau:
http://www.museum-poteau44.be/
December 44 Museum, La Gleize: http://www.december44.com/
Malmédy Massacre Museum, Baugnez: http://www.baugnez44.be/
Battle of the Bulge Museum, La Roche-en-Ardenne:
http://www.batarden.be/
National Museum of Military History, Diekirch:
http://www.mnhm.lu/pageshtml/museumprofile.php

## Military Cemeteries

Henri-Chapelle Cemetery in Hombourg near Liège has 8,000 graves, including many US Air Force airmen. Neuville-en-Condroz Cemetery, southwest of Liège has 5,000 graves, many from the battle of Aachen. The American Cemetery in Luxembourg has another 5,000 graves, including that of General George S. Patton, who died following a car accident in December 1945. The German Military Cemetery is at Recogne, just outside Bastogne.

# FURTHER READING

Bruning, John R., *The Battle of the Bulge: The Photographic History of an American Triumph* (Zenith Press, 2009)

Cole, Hugh M., *The Ardennes: The Official History of the Battle of the Bulge* (Red and Black Publishers)

Cross, R., *The Battle of the Bulge 1944: Hitler's Last Hope* (The History Press, 2002)

Eisenhower John S.D., *The Bitter Woods: The Battle of the Bulge* (Da Capo Press, 1995)

Green, Michael, *War Stories of the Battle of the Bulge* (Zenith Press, 2010)

MacDonald, Charles B., *A Time for Trumpets: The Untold Story of the Battle of the Bulge* (Harper Perennial, 1997)

Pallud, Jean-Paul, *Battle of the Bulge: Then and Now* (After the Battle Magazine, 1986)

Parker, Danny S., *Battle of the Bulge: Hitler's Ardennes Offensive, 1944–1945* (Da Capo Press, 2004)

Toland, John and Carlo D'Este, *Battle: The Story of the Bulge* (Bison Books, 1999)

Tout, K., *An End of War: Fatal Final Days to VE Day 1945* (The History Press 2011)

Whiting, C., *Patton's Last Battle* (The History Press 1999)

Winton, Harold R., *Corps Commanders of the Bulge: Six American Generals and Victory in the Ardennes* (University Press of Kansas, 2007)

Zagola, Steven, *Battle of the Bulge* (Osprey Publishing, 2010)

# INDEX

# Index

# Index

# Index